C000179458

SEAFARERS' VOICES 10

Rolling Home

ROLLING HOME

William Morris Barnes

Edited with an introduction by
Vincent McInerney

Seaforth
PUBLISHING

This edition copyright © A Vincent McInerney 2013

First published in Great Britain in 2013 by
Seaforth Publishing,
Pen & Sword Books Ltd,
47 Church Street,
Barnsley S70 2AS

www.seaforthpublishing.com

British Library Cataloguing in Publication Data
A catalogue record for this book
is available from the British Library
ISBN 978 1 84832 165 6

Typeset and designed by M.A.T.S. Leigh-on-Sea, Essex
Printed and bound in Great Britain
by CPI Group (UK) Ltd, Croydon, CR0 4YY

Contents

Contents

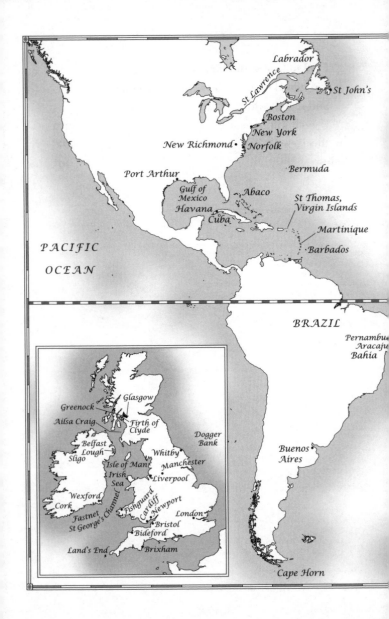

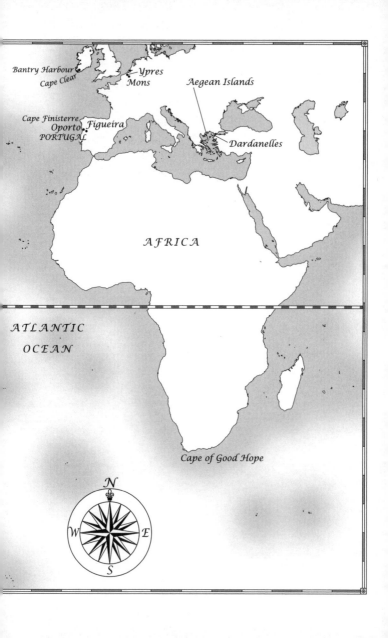

Editorial Note

THIS ABRIDGED EDITION is based on the 1931 English edition of *Rolling Home: When Ships were Ships and Not Tin Pots*, published by Cassell & Co, London. An American edition had appeared a year earlier under the title of *When Ships were Ships and Not Tin Pots: The Seafaring Adventures of Captain William Morris Barnes*, published by Albert & Charles Boni, New York.

The American edition differs from the English one in having a foreword and a dedication to Hilda Wortman, wife of the New York cartoonist Denys Wortman.[1] It was she who came across Barnes in Greenwich Village and, taken by his wild look and his language, befriended him and encouraged him to retell his experiences. This colourful sailor was also to enthuse Denys Wortman, and Barnes became the inspiration for one of Wortman's most popular and memorable cartoon characters, Mopey Dick, a working-class New Yorker who would comment on the city and on important matters of the day.

Editorial Note

Hilda Wortman, meanwhile, was transcribing the stories that Barnes had recounted into a tape recorder, and it is these transcriptions, carefully converted from word to text, that make up *Rolling Home.* It is a peculiarity of the English edition that no credit is given to Wortman's input; perhaps the publishers thought that her editorship somehow lessened the authenticity of the author's voice. But the fact is, it was her recognition of Barnes's storytelling ability that was to lead to this most remarkable of seaman's memoirs.

Introduction

> You sailor lads of Liverpool,
> you rambling boys take care!
> If you sign a 'Bluenose' merchantman,
> no dungaree jumpers wear.
> But keep a monkey jacket
> close under your command,
> For there blow some sharp nor'westers
> off the Banks of Newfoundland.
> Oh, we'll wash her and we'll scrub her down,
> with holystone and sand;
> Then we'll be gone from cold St John,
> and the Banks of Newfoundland.
>
> Fo'c'sle verse

Captain William Morris Barnes (1850–1934) was born into an affluent St John's, Newfoundland, shipowning family where he would have heard little but seafaring matters discussed daily from childhood. St John's was the largest city in Newfoundland, dependent on the sealing and fishing industries. Cod were bountiful, while seal kills during the annual seal hunt were by the time of Barnes's birth averaging half a million tons. Conditions were harsh, winters long, and Barnes would have acquired a toughness of mind and body during his early years, and his later seagoing career was based on what might be termed rugged individualism, plus a robust physical approach to all shipboard problems from monsoons to mutineers, which enabled him to rise from lowly ship's boy to captain.

He spent most of his life at sea in a career that spanned the transition from sail to steam in the second part of the nineteenth century. In many ways, the trajectory of his career was typical, even ordinary in the context of the times, but the fact that his autobiography makes such riveting reading shows how much more exotic was the life of a sailor than the average land-lubber. *Rolling Home* offers the reader a spellbinding collection of sailor's yarns in which the author relates not so much a career narrative as an episodic tale of adventure, danger and hardship. His turn of phrase is sharp and salty – he relates how his mother-in-law 'hates him like the devil hates holy water' – while the opening lines of the chapters never fail to draw the reader quickly in. 'Did I ever tell you I went adrift in a horse and carriage? It was the dirtiest night that ever came out of the heavens', begins one. Exaggeration, such a key ingredient of many seamen's yarns, is never far away. In Barnes's case it heightens the drama of his extraordinary career, but also, because of the manner in which the tales were retold by his editor Hilda Wortman, reflects the way the seaman was beheld by his land-bound contemporaries: a rough and colourful figure, adrift in the unfathomable and mysterious world of ships and distant seas.

Barnes first went to sea while still a schoolboy. His career seemed predestined, and by the age of fourteen he was apprenticed to a Liverpool company, serving in their sailing ships working a triangular passage to St John's, the Brazils, and back to Liverpool. He tried to 'swallow the anchor' when he married, but life as a uxorious husband running a grocery store was too mundane, and he soon went back to sea, transferring his skills to the now dominant steamships.

So much was the life of a seafarer in his bones that even late in his career, at the age sixty-four, a time when most men would have been looking forward to a snug berth onshore, he promptly volunteered for service on the outbreak of the First World War. He does not seem to have regretted it, even after being mined and torpedoed four times, once being badly injured and spending three days adrift in an open boat. Despite these disasters, like many a sailor, he was probably safer at sea – whilst ashore during the war he fell deeply in love with a woman, attracted partly by her air of mystery, soon to discover, however, that she was a German spy and he only narrowly escaped arrest as an accessory to the fact.

He led an adventurous and peril-bound existence, which is a common thread leading through so many mariners' memoirs, but what makes Barnes's book possibly unique within seafaring accounts is the amount of space that women occupy within his volume, especially the length of time he spends discussing both his courtship and marriage, his relationship with his wife and girlfriend, and also the position of dock-road women in the life of a sailor. There are many volumes of *Letters To ...* from naval captains and commanders to their wives, but in the merchant service there seems to be far less extant material to or about wives, home life, and families.

Another rare aspect to his book is that Barnes gives us his life until his eightieth year. Most memoirs by seafarers finish when their sea careers end, often at a young age. Anything beyond the end of a sailor's career is usually drawn from the reminiscences of others, conjecture, or historical research. With Barnes we have his own recorded thoughts almost until his death at eighty-five. 'Are you prepared to die?' asks a friend at the end of the book. 'Prepared?' says I. 'I was always prepared. I've been prepared since the first day I went to sea. ... I wasn't afraid. If you don't know a sailor's religion, I'll tell it to you and this is my religion: a clear conscience, a sharp knife and ready to cut out at a moment's notice.'

Barnes begins *Rolling Home* by painting a picture of himself as a boy in St John's. The first recorded visit to

Introduction

St John's was by the Italian navigator Giovanni Caboto (John Cabot) who, under letters patent of Henry VII, is said to have sailed into its harbour on 24 June 1497, the feast day of John the Baptist – hence the port's name. It later had a heavy influx of English West Country seamen, mainly from Devon (ie, from one fishing area to another), and these, plus Irish immigrants, developed St John's into the world-renowned centre of the cod trade.

An account of the city written close to the time of Barnes's birth (1850) gives a lively overview:

Trying to describe St John's, there is some difficulty finding an adjective ... Other cities are coupled with words which give predominant characteristics: London the richest, Paris the gayest, etc ... But in one respect St John has no rival: – 'the fishiest'. Round the harbour are acres of sheds roofed with cod split in half, laid on like slates, drying in the sun. Stout weatherly ships, bearing nearly every flag in the world, crowd up to the wharves laden with cod. The few scant fields of cultivation are manured with cod. The trim wooden houses, their handsome furniture, the piano, and the musical skill of the young lady who plays it, are all paid for in cod. In fact, there seems only one place which appears to be sacred from its intrusion, and that is the dinner table. ... There are also the seal fisheries which employ numbers of active and experienced sailors in the more Northern Seas; lives of incredible hardship and danger.

The town itself is irregular and dirty, built chiefly of wood; a large fish oil factory in the centre filling the air with most obnoxious odours. The heavy rains plough the streets into water courses. Thousands of lean dogs stalk about, quarrelling for fish offal – scattered in all directions. This is their recreation: their business is to draw go-carts. There are also great numbers of cats, which, on account of the dogs, generally reside on the tops of the houses. The population of the island is one hundred thousand; one half are Roman Catholics, principally of Irish descent, or emigrants; the remainder of English race and various creeds.

But if St John's be the fishiest, it is also one of the friendliest places in the world; no cold, formal, letter-of-introduction dinners, but hearty, cordial, and agreeable hospitality. Society, of course, is limited. The clergy, the civil and military officers. Also the principal merchants – men of affluence, kindness, intelligence, and instructive and agreeable views. Among the younger members of their families, not a few have had European education.[2]

The writer, George Warburton, also details the incredible density of cod off Newfoundland:

Reaching Portugal Cove, we found the inn to be a small wooden building with a view of a waterfall. Said to be a favourite spot for honeymooners; and perhaps judiciously chosen as there is nothing else whatever of luxury, convenience, or amusement, to disturb the thoughts of the happy couple from each other. ... We embarked a rough clumsy boat and pulled towards a large flat island. Off the end of this was a rock, like one of the round towers of Ireland, rising to about two hundred yards above the sea. Our wild boatman, speaking in a Cork brogue overlaid with Yankee twang, said that no one, barring the birds, had ever got to the top of it. The Captain's reply was that unless the inducements to get there were very much increased, probably none ever would.

We cast out our lines – containing three or four hooks baited with slices of fish. Within a minute we were pulling up our prizes, pale distorted ghosts of sea monsters which, as they neared the surface, condensed into exhausted and resigned codfish which soon had their sufferings rapidly brought to an end by their being struck on the head with a short bludgeon called 'The Priest.' After that, pieces of the tail of one were cut off to furnish fresh bait and such were their cannibal propensities we soon caught so many that we were heartily tired of the sport.[3]

Barnes's account also makes evident what is also an established meteorological truth – that St John's, of all major Canadian cities, is the foggiest, snowiest, wettest, windiest, cloudiest, and although the climate is designated 'mild' for eastern Canada, winters can be severe.

The history of the Barnes family on both sides was Irish. Paternally, Barnes's great-grandfather, after almost being hanged by the English, escaped to America via France and then moved into Canada after the American Revolutionary War (1775–83). Settling in St John's he bought a boat and began to deal in fish and to make money, his sons buying two boats and expanding the business. Maternally, the great-grandfather, surname Allen, was an Irish immigrant who began as a sealer. Migratory fishermen began hunting seals in the region of Newfoundland and Labrador and the Gulf of St Lawrence in the 1500s, leading to the Newfoundland seal hunt, an annual event from 1723. By the time of Barnes's birth, seal kills were averaging about half a million tons. In the 1870s the industry was transformed by the arrival of large, steam-powered sealing vessels, and by the late nineteenth century the Newfoundland sealing industry was second in importance only to the cod.

The other source of income for the Barnes/Allen family was the shipping of emigrants from Ireland. With the end of the second American war in 1814, the Irish, still under British rule, were attracted by the potential freedom and opportunity America offered. From the 1820s onward, immigration to North America expanded exponentially. This diaspora increased with the advent of the Irish famine in 1845 which saw even more of the indigenous population attempting to flee, although many did not survive the passage:

Introduction

The Montreal Immigrant Committee, in 1847, states
the year has been unparalleled for immigration into
Canada. Nearly 100,000 souls left the British Isles;
over 5,000 died on the passage out; 3,389 at Grosse
Isle; 3,862 at Montreal; and other places saw the same
fearful proportions. Never had Canada presented
such fearful scenes of destitution and suffering. From
Grosse Isle, that great charnel-house for victimised
humanity, and wherever the tide of immigration has
extended, are to be found the final resting places of
the sons and daughters of Erin – one unbroken chain
of graves, where repose fathers and mothers, sisters
and brothers, in one commingled heap.[4]

So much had the Barnes family's seafaring ventures
prospered, that by the time Barnes was a boy, the family
were employing three maids, a seamstress, and a
combined major-domo/male servant of all work/
coachman, called Richard Mahoney. According to his
account, Barnes idolised Mahoney, who encouraged him
in his youthful days to fight other boys on every occasion,
a cultivated aggression which paid real dividends later as
Barnes tells us, 'Once you become an officer – well, unless
you can use your fists, you might as well look for a
thousand dollars in the street as look for a mate's berth.'

We are told that at age eleven, Barnes (by using his
mother's intercession) persuaded his father to allow him
to make a trip in a family vessel, the *Fleetwing*, to
Pernambuco. He returned, now firmly set on the sea,

only to find the family firm bankrupt through over-extending credit. The family had to move house, and Barnes attended the local school, where he caused many problems, even throwing a slate at the master which narrowly missed the man's head and stuck in the blackboard 'an inch and a half'. After being withdrawn he recommenced his seafaring career as a 'Boy' on the *Mary*, on the St John's–Pernambuco–Liverpool–St John's run. In the course of this voyage a man was lost overboard, and we learn for the first time of Barnes' lifelong belief in the paranormal – not unusual in seamen of that period. This run was eventually the one with which Barnes identified most closely for the rest of his time sailing out of Canada. Some seamen, early in their careers, find a run whose length, plus the ports visited, suit them in such a manner that nothing else is really sought. The 'packet rats' with their Liverpool/New York/Liverpool would sail nothing else:

> ... one of his boasts was he had sailed in the Packets for five years and never seen the pay table. He would sign on in Liverpool giving his boarding-master his month's advance note for quittance. At New York he would desert, and after a bout ashore, would sail for Liverpool again in a new ship. 'None of yer slaving at cargo for me!' he would explain. 'Ah wos a sailorman and only did sailoring jobs. Them wos the days w'en sailors were men, an' not the ruddy cargo-wrestlin', coal-diggin' scallywags wot they be now!'[5]

Favoured runs like the 'MANZ' (Montreal–Australia–
New Zealand) at ten months, with its attendant large
pay-off, were also much sought after by those saving to
marry. But for Barnes, St John's–the 'Brazils'–Liverpool
was the run about which he speaks most, and where his
heart seemed to be, although he did also go 'East', and
records one such trip in his book.

After a second trip as 'Boy', Barnes, aged fourteen
and a half, began a four and a half year apprenticeship
on the ship *Miranda*. During these years, in Liverpool,
he met Edward Smith who was to be captain of the ill-
fated *Titanic*. Smith was himself an apprentice at that
time. Barnes also began to learn the hard facts of the
sailor's life both at sea and ashore. In these years in and
out of Liverpool, he also had his first encounters with
the women who, at that time, frequented the dock roads
of the great ports of the world. Up to the time of the
huge expansion of container ships at the end of the
1960s, when a fortnight or three alongside became only
a distant memory, the relationships between dock road
women and sailors had been relatively unchanged for
two hundred years. Everyone knew what was available;
how much it cost; what you got for your money; and
how long and on what terms such a relationship would
last. In the 1840s, Liverpool, with its murky past of
privateering and slaving, was infamous for its women,
as the traditional sailor's foc's'le verse indicates: 'When
I paid-off in Liverpool twas up the Frederick Street /

Where I espied a pretty barque by name of *Bridget Fleet*
/ Oh, the waves they do crash! And the winds they do
roar! /And at each house in Canning Place there stands
a whore!'

Melville, in *Redburn*, sets the tone:

> Of all sea-ports, Liverpool, perhaps, most abounds
> in all varieties of land-sharks, land-rats, and other
> vermin who devour the hapless mariner. But other
> perils he runs, far worse; from the denizens of those
> notorious *Corinthian* haunts in the vicinity of the
> docks; which, in depravity, are not to be matched this
> side of the bottomless pit. And yet sailors love this
> Liverpool; and upon long voyages will be continually
> dilating upon its charms and attractions, and
> extolling it above all other sea-ports in the world. For
> in Liverpool they find their Paradise – not the well
> known street of that name – and one of them told me
> he would be content to lie in Prince's Dock till *he hove
> up anchor* for the world to come.[6]

Out of his apprenticeship, leaving the *Miranda*, Barnes
shipped in the *Jane*, a Newfoundland 'fish-box' carrying
barrels of salt-cod to 'the Brazils'. In the 1860s, together
with the China tea clippers, the Newfoundland fish-
boxes were considered the hardest-driven ships afloat,
'because both had to run for market.' The first fish-box
of the season that arrived in Pernambuco would
command the best prices for its cargo. As with the tea
clippers, there were heavy bets laid, up to £500. The

captain of the successful vessel would get 'fifty dollars; the profit off fifty drums of fish; and a new beaver hat.' Barnes' ship was first, though only by the ploy of rowing two barrels of fish (as a sample) eight miles into Pernambuco harbour when the *Jane* and its rival, the *Meteor*, both became becalmed.

Barnes advanced to the rank of mate, and after a number of adventures, including a bout of yellow fever, and being jailed for attempting to drown two soldiers, he passed for captain, gaining his certificate of competency on 31 December 1876, aged twenty-six. Certificates were brought in on British vessels in 1850, following the Merchant Seaman's Act of 1845. Up to that time masters and mates could be appointed by 'giving references to the owners of their former vessels when seeking employment'.[7] This was why many captains could neither read nor navigate. Anglesey, for instance, was known as 'the banister to Ireland' because captains of ships for Dublin from Liverpool would 'feel' their way around that island to Holyhead, and then head due west across the Irish Sea with little to guide them but the hope in their hearts. Certification did not immediately follow in the British colonies, and Barnes, taking a ship from St John's to Greenock as captain, encountered problems as the old informalities clashed with the new regulated system, when port authorities in Scotland would not accept his status as master due to his lack of 'papers'.

We see Barnes' self-confidence and optimism when he takes on the *Corinne* – which had a continual leak and from which the previous two captains had walked away – in spite of detecting that the leak was due to Toredo worms which enter underwater but 'don't bore straight as you would with a gimlet – they bore like a snake walks and from where they enter to where they come out on the inside might be five feet. It might also enter as a small worm but by the time it eats its way though those five feet it will be a big worm and cause a big leak.' These worms had caused problems on wooden ships since time immemorial, with methods of prevention being sought and prescribed with an almost alchemical fervour:

> TAKE a hundred pounds weight of the finest pitch, (the stuff or mixture which is used in the painting of ships' bottoms) melt it over a slow and steady fire of charcoal. When it is thoroughly melted, add to it thirty pounds of roll brimstone, grossly braised; and boil the whole over a charcoal fire till thirty pounds are wasted. ... The scum to be continually taken off, as in the boiling of sugar, lest it should rise above the brim of the pot. But if rising cannot be prevented, you may quell it by throwing into it a lump of soot.[8]

In captaining the *Corinne* to Boston, Barnes not only almost lost it from the worm leak and had to quell a mutiny, but at Boston was cheated out of the bulk of his wages, getting only thirty-two dollars instead of four hundred. However, this was not the last of his adventures and he made the passage into 'steam' when he took an officer's job in SS *Korona*. At the time Barnes sailed in her she still belonged to the Quebec Steamship Company, although Furness Withy did eventually come to own the *Korona* through acquisition.

In the spring of 1914 Barnes joined one of Houston Line vessels, the *Herminius*, and was in Liverpool when war was declared. When the First World War broke out, Canada had little in the way of a merchant marine – the Canadian Navy itself 'consisted of fewer than 350 men and two old ships.' Canada and Britain, therefore, decided that Canada's war effort would be best concentrated on the army. But although her merchant fleet was negligible, and seen as being spurious to needs, many Canadian and Newfoundland sailors felt it was their duty to volunteer and came to Britain to do so. Barnes was one of these volunteers, as were two of his sons, one in the army and the other a sea captain. The army son is said by Barnes to have been part of the Robert Peary (1856–1920) expedition of 1909 to the North Pole, and certainly a John Barnes appears on the crew list.

Although told that, at sixty-four, he was 'the oldest man to have come across from the other side', Barnes was appointed second officer on the *Moreus* and a week later he was mined off Malta. During the war Barnes was also torpedoed twice: one of these ships was the steamer *Inverbervie* (built by Russell in 1913, Rowat SS Co) and torpedoed by KuK (Austro-Hungarian) *U4* off Cape Rizzuto. Barnes was also torpedoed in the *Saxonian* by *U39*, incurring a face wound, and then a hernia while climbing into the lifeboat, which was adrift for three days before being picked up by a British destroyer.

Barnes' final wartime posting was to a small fishing craft, the *Mary*, fitted out as a decoy, or Q-ship. These were vessels that were armed but designed to look innocuous – the very embodiment of the 'wolf in sheep's clothing'. Submarines were wreaking havoc on shipping, and depth charges were primitive. Almost the only chance of sinking a submarine was by surface gunfire or ramming on the surface, but the problem was luring the U-boat to the surface – hence the bait of the Q-ships, with their outward appearance as ostensibly easy targets. As it turned out, the *Mary* was torpedoed and sunk off Whitby, though Barnes succeeded in sailing over and possibly sinking the U-boat just before *Mary* disappeared beneath the waves.

Barnes finally retired to a berth in Snug Harbor, which had been founded in 1801 on the north shore of Staten Island as a home for aged sailors by Captain Robert Richard Randall. In New York Barnes got to know a couple called Hilda and Denys Wortman. Denys was a newspaper cartoonist, who was rather taken with the gruff old sea-dog, and based a character he dubbed

'Mopey Dick' on him for a series of popular cartoons.
Meanwhile, Hilda encouraged Barnes to record his
adventures and she eventually became the editor of the
first edition of this book, imbuing the story with far
more narrative flair than might usually be found in such
unliterary memoirs. However, not all the skill was hers;
oral storytelling was an important part of the sailor's
life and Barnes retold the stories of his life at sea in a
way that captured her imagination. Hilda Wortman's
great contribution was to recognise the quality of this
storytelling and set down, not a conventional
autobiography, but a unique and marvellous series of
sailor's yarns.

Barnes began oil painting – 'Some I sell, more I give
away,' and tells us his father's first cousin was 'the great
William Morris of London. At home in St John's we had
paintings of my grandfather and Uncle Richard and
Uncle John by William Morris', but history does not
record whether this was just another seaman's yarn.

Barnes, although sailing as a captain for long
periods, always comes across as 'one of the crowd'.
There is always the feeling that, after coming down
from the bridge, it would not be the passenger saloon
Barnes would make for, but the foc's'le. He was eighty
or more when he wrote *Rolling Home*. Certain people,
at no matter what advanced age they die, are always
seventeen and waiting for life to begin. Barnes is of
this company.

Rolling Home

1. Birth – life in St John's, Newfoundland – my first trip to sea aged eleven – I finish early with school.

TO BEGIN. I came into this world at midnight on 3 February 1850, during the worst storm known in St John's, Newfoundland, in sixty years. Even so, my mother and aunt later told me I made more noise than what was going on outside. The midwife said, 'The child is hungry', went out, got a saucer of bread and milk, and I ate the whole of it. They said when I was born I had black hair on my head nearly an inch long.

Growing up, we had an Irish coachman called Richard Mahoney. I thought that there was no one like Richard – and Richard liked me. Whenever he was on the street on an errand for my father or mother I would be with him.

'Will', he would say to me, as we were going along, 'Do you think you can beat that fellow?' That was all I wanted. I'd go over and have a fight with whoever it was. Sometimes I would get more than I bargained for, but most times I came out best. One day I got fighting with a boy who gave me the hell of a licking, and I came home with my face all cut up.

My mother said, 'Did Richard put you up to it?' I didn't answer. When my father came in, she told him, and he called me over.

'Who started it?'

'I did.'

'Did Richard tell you to do it?'

'No.' He sent me out, and called in Richard. And thinking I'd told, Richard admitted it. But I never would have told.

At that time, Richard was thirty-six and a damn fine looking man – especially in his tall beaver hat and long coat with brass buttons. We had three serving girls in that house, plus a seamstress, Kate Carey, who would sit with my mother all day making dresses. In those days, even a rich woman wouldn't buy ready-made clothes. Well, Kate fell in love with Richard, and he fell in love with her, and they got married. After he died, and she was getting older, whenever any of our family passed away Kate would do the honours. The washing, laying out, and fixing them – she being Irish Catholic.

Now for my family history. My great-grandfather was born in Waterford, Ireland. They were fighting then, trying to free Ireland from England, and they lost a battle and my great-grandfather was taken prisoner. They led his horse under a tree, tied his hands behind his back, put a noose over a branch and round his neck, lashed the stirrups under the horse's belly, and left him there. They thought as soon as they went the horse would move to crop grass – leaving my great-grandfather to swing. My father said my great-grandfather was there an hour and the horse never moved. Then some of his own party came along, released him, and they decided to escape from Ireland. They stole a boat, and in St George's Channel were picked up by some French fishermen – no lovers of the British. From France my great-grandfather came to America.

Three years afterwards, Washington took arms against the British and, of course, my great-grandfather joined Washington. My great-grandfather's brother went second or third lieutenant on the *Randolph*, frigate. They had only six frigates at the time. Later, after he left her, the *Randolph*'s powder magazine blew up and I believe nearly all were killed.

After the peace was made, people began travelling all over – into Canada and out of Canada – and my great-grandfather went to Canada. There, hearing great reports of Newfoundland, went out and settled in St John's. He began a little fishing business that made money, and when he died my grandfather carried on and bought two vessels – the *Royal William* and the *Angler*, both brigs, and when my grandfather died he left them to my father and my uncle John.

That was my father's family. My mother was an Allen. Her father was 'Old Tom' Allen – a hard old Irish

23

rooster! He came out in what they call an emigrant ship; a well-educated man in the days when very few Irishmen were educated. Would you believe it? Some of the Newfoundland Irish were so ignorant they hated their own children because they weren't born in Ireland – calling them 'God-damned bush born!'

Well, my grandfather could navigate, and made money, and bought a brig called the *Shaver*. With fifty men he went as a sealer. Of course, my Allen grandmother didn't like it, because, like all Irishmen, he would play cards after bringing home a load of seals. He would spend a lot of the money, but she would take most and put it in property and land. And when the seal fishery was over for the year, he would clean the ship and go across to Cork and bring back loads of emigrants to Newfoundland and New York.

Then he bought the *Sally*; and did the same. In the summer he would go down to Labrador, the two vessels full of 'freighters'– passengers who went there to fish. He had his own place on the Labrador. In the fall of the year, they would bring back the fish to St John's and sell it on the wharves. He made money hand over fist, and my grandmother put it into land and houses, and this went on until, like almost all old sealing captains, he went blind. That comes from being up the mast in the look-out barrel gazing over ice seas. When he went blind, every day, three times a day, my grandfather would have his grog. If he didn't get it, hell was in the house. His wife would give it him, he would take as long as he could to drink it, then look at her – his eyes were always open and you would think he could see – and say, 'You didn't forget to put plenty of water in that.'

My grandfather was hard. One time on the seal fishery his ship got crushed in an ice field. Before she went down, they got the grub and everything, plus some sails, onto a floe. They sighted this big berg coming along – nice, flat, and deep. Bergs don't sink as quick as the field ice, and go through it just like a steamer. So now they cut handholds in the berg with the axes, and got up with all their barrels of beef, pork, and everything else. The only thing they forgot was a stove. The next thing was to take the sails they had rescued, and some spars, and make tents on top of the iceberg. Very low tents – otherwise the wind would blow them away. They were eighteen days on that berg, driving south all the time, and were almost back at St John's before being taken off and brought in.

There's a great big Roman Catholic chapel in St John's, St Patrick's, one of the finest on this side of the Atlantic. When they were building it, all the old sealers took their crews to the south side of St John's where there was a big quarry, and they carved out rocks and put them on sleighs to haul them back to the cathedral to help build it, their own ship's flags flying above their sleighs, and the men singing shanties. Then they'd go into the woods and haul out great big trees they would peel and clean, each captain putting them in their own pile. My grandfather brought out two huge trees. That night, Old Mullins, another captain, an ignorant old clown, told his men to substitute my grandfather's two spars. But my grandfather's crew knew every tree they'd cut and next morning told my grandfather. My grandfather made a run at Mullins, at the same time calling on his own men to take back the spars.

Who comes down but Bishop Fleming. 'What's the matter here? What's all this about?'

My grandfather says, 'Bishop Fleming, last night this damn fellow and his crew stole two of the spars I'd cut for your church.'

'You lie,' said Mullen.

'No.' said my grandfather. 'You lie!'

'Now look here, Allen,' Bishop Fleming says. 'Never mind about the spars – let them lay.' You see, Fleming knew my grandfather was the most unliked the man of the two, because my grandfather was educated.

'Damned if I will!' said my grandfather

'Go home and stop all this!' Fleming now says. 'I say to you to do this.'

'No. I won't!'

'Well,' says Fleming, 'I never want to see your face again.' Then he made some sort of sign, like they generally do, thinking to frighten my grandfather.

But all my grandfather said was, 'Damned if I ever

see your face again! While you're preaching in that chapel I'll never darken its door!'

Shortly after, the chapel was finished enough to have masses said, but my grandfather wouldn't go there, no matter how ragged by the family – not until the day Bishop Fleming died. Then my grandfather dressed up in his best and went to the church. That'll show you the kind of 'Old Hairpins' they had at that time, those old Irish captains. Pretty hard tickets. And my Allen grandfather was one of them – hard as a rock.

Now a word about religions. If I had my way, I'd issue a proclamation that all churches should be made into one – don't call it Roman Catholic, or Protestant or anything else. Because, as a boy, I watched all the squabbling and fightings between those two churches, how they'd even tell their congregations not to go to the other because then they'd be sent to hell. No, I'd have one universal church called 'The Church of God' – and I believe there would be lots of Catholics and Protestants would race to that church and be very glad. And all those that objected going there could worship as they like – even my own children – let them carry their own opinions out into the world. As for myself, if I want to pray, I do it in my own room. I don't go out with a big book under my arm to let people see me. And when we die – well, then we'll find out who was right or wrong. People might think, hearing me talking, I'm an atheist. Well, I've read as much as the next; studied the churches and their goings-on all my life: hypocrisies and miseries in all of them. So every night I generally say my prayers in my own room – what I was taught by my mother, the Lord's Prayer. But if I've made a heavy bet on the races I offer up a particular prayer, especially when I'd have nothing left if I lost. And often I'd pray special in a big gale when the hatches might be stove in, and we'd go down. But more than once I didn't pray in that sort of danger because I was too busy swearing.

When my grandfather Allen died, my grandmother owned a great big estate. It was called Allen's Square with houses all around, and a big hill running down into the town called Allen's Hill. And when she died, my mother and father married and now the two families, Barnes and Allen, combined their interests, run by my father and my uncle John. They began to advance supplies to fishermen, and when the fish was brought home, they'd salt it and ship it to the West Indies. And when they'd sell the fish, down in Barbados, they'd sail to Cuba and load molasses or sugar or rum, which they'd bring home at good profit. In the end they had thirteen sail, and the business so big they both had to stay onshore. They built this beautiful barque, the *Fleetwing*, so fast nothing ever got to her. She was built at Green Bay, Newfoundland, by a man called Newhook. They couldn't get the pitch-pine masts they wanted down there, so brought her up under jury masts to St John's, where she was fitted out by John Knight, head ship's carpenter, and another man called John Marshall, who, as a powder boy, fought alongside Nelson at the Battle of Trafalgar.

The *Fleetwing*'s first trip was to Pernambuco, Brazil, which she made in thirty-two days under Captain Robert Knight, brother of the head carpenter. When they got back Knight said there was nothing the *Fleetwing* didn't come up with and pass, while nothing ever passed him.

Now I had my holidays, and asked my mother to ask my father to let me go on a voyage. The *Fleetwing* was again loading for the Brazils, and he agreed. I was out of my mind with excitement! I got an old wooden sailor's chest and spend all my time packing and unpacking: sea-boots, an oilcoat and pants, a blue knitted sailor's Guernsey, a canvas jumper, a belt and sheath knife. I was as proud as a peacock going round for two days wishing all my friends and relations goodbye, and then I came to wish my mother and father goodbye. I was eleven years old. My poor mother had tears in her eyes, my father shook my hand. Mother gave me about £12 English money, more than plenty. When we got outside the 'Heads', the ship began to jump, and it was not long before I was sick as could be. I was sick about five days. Then I was able to get around, but could not eat anything. The cook said, 'Billy, if you want to get well quick, get a small piece of fat pork with the string on, swallow it, then haul it up again.' This made me twice as sick as before. One day the captain caught him at this and gave him a sock on the jaw which knocked him over.

The captain said, 'You damn skunk. Don't you think the boy is sick enough?'

When I finally got on deck properly, I thought I was in heaven. Climbing aloft everywhere, up and around the yards like a monkey. Then, in the evening dog watches, with the men sitting round telling yarns, I'd be right in the middle. And I believed it all.

The captain said, 'Look here, Bill, your father will give me fits. He told me to keep you clear of the sailors, so as not to learn any badness.'

'Captain, there is no badness,' I told him. 'Everything I hear is good – all about splices and such.'

'Oh, well, that won't hurt you.' But he knew darn well they used to swear. At that time I thought it was an awful thing – in fact, I never got broken into swearing until I got to be an officer – not even when I was before the mast. But when I got to be an officer, and got charge, if the men weren't doing exactly what I liked the first thing to come out of me would be an oath. And even now, even in decent company, out it comes when I'm excited – telling a story or anything. But I'm not committing a sin. Because I don't know I'm swearing, see? I know a lot of people say, 'That seems an ill-bred fellow. Where was he dragged up?' And my father, even when I was a man, he'd say,

'You're not in a fight in a brothel now. Keep decent while you're here.'

However, back on board the *Fleetwing*, everything went right until we got to the equator and Neptune came over the bows and asked if there was any of his children to be baptised. The captain said, 'Two,' – a fellow called Jim Brown, and myself. Of course, I immediately flew aloft – so they started to shave the other fellow, lathering him with tar and grease, and using a peace of rusty old iron with a jagged edge for the razor. He kicked and roared like the town bull. Then they dumped him into a tub of saltwater and scrubbed him with deck brushes. Then they called me to come down. I said I would not and now Neptune himself, a terrible-looking object, his head nothing but a mass of white hair that came down early to his knees, and his whole body covered with knives and daggers – now he pointed a big revolver at me and I came down and they shaved me just as the other fellow. Then he wished us goodbye and went over the bows, and later the captain said, 'Go down to my room and watch yourself,' and I saw Neptune's revolver in his room and understood all.

Every day, while in the southern tradewinds, I was out on the end of the flying jibboom trying to catch dolphins with the 'grains' – an iron with four prongs like a fork, with a beard on the end of each tine, which will hold to the fish when you drive it in. A dolphin is about three or four feet long, and when you catch it, and it is dying on the deck, it changes into all sorts of colours like a rainbow.

We arrived in Pernambuco in thirty-five days. The cargo sold well, and I had a great time. The consignee, an Englishman named Saunders, invited me to his home where there were two boys and a girl near my age. Every day we were off in his wagon, driving all over the country, through the sugar plantations, eating all kinds of fruit. When we left I had a cabin full of presents for my mother and father, and a monkey, parrot, and marmoset for myself. Going home it was coming on winter. We had very bad weather, nothing but gales and winter seas, mountains high. One man broke his leg, and the captain had to fix it in splints. After thirty-seven days we got to St John's with the loss of some sails and spars.

Anyway, I got back to find the firm in slings. My father and uncle John had advanced supplies to the fishermen while the fish were swimming in the sea, and it had been a very bad year for the fish. The merchants bought on three months' notice, and bills were coming in from New York in the West Indies and everywhere. They called a meeting of creditors and when everything was examined, most creditors were for letting my father and uncle go, as they had the assets of the ships and fishing schooners. But there was an old Scots merchant by the name of Grieve who was owed more than anyone else who wouldn't have it. So my father got reckless and

said, 'Take it all and be damned with the whole lot.'
Well, it took three years to wind up the business and
they paid nineteen shillings in the pound, so they were
not really failures. The next year the fish were eating
rocks, they were so plentiful, and my father told me that
if they had not had to fail, they would have made
another small fortune. But as it was the ships and horses
were sold off – even my little pony and carriage was
sold. When they were taking my pony away I hung on
to his tail trying to it hold back crying and roaring, and
my father had to haul me away.

So now we had to move to a new house, while I went
to the Academy and got mixed up with the boys in
town. One was Tom Powers, a great fellow for all kinds
of risky business. One day we were at the courthouse,
the largest building on Water Street, five or six stories
high, built of large blocks of stone with an inlet around
and between each about an inch wide and deep – just
enough for the tips of our fingers and boots.

Power says to me, 'We'll go up and write our names
under the clock. Have you a pencil?'

'Yes,' I says, 'In my pocket.'

He was about eight feet from me and we started up
like two spiders, block after block. It was about seven of
a summer's evening, and as the shops were open in
Water Street till ten them days, soon the whole city was
out to see us. The policeman came along and no one
was to sing out to us as we would be sure to fall. Finally,

we got to the clock, and Power wrote his name on one side of the clock, and I wrote mine on the other side, each holding on with one hand. Then we came down, and were nabbed at once, and taken to the police house. They put both of us in the same cell, but we were hardly there a moment when my father came in. At that time he was a big bug in St John's.

He says to the policeman, 'Let him out. I'll give him more punishment than the law.' The police were delighted. My father yanked me home by the collar, and brought me up to the nursery. We had a nurse then, a young woman called Joanna.

'Joanna,' he says, 'Hand me that switch.' She brought it over with tears in her eyes, then went out. And right in the middle of the floor he gave it to me. There were stripes on my shoulders for three days after, the worst licking he ever gave me. I got one or two other beatings off my father, but those were with his fists.

Then another night myself, Tom Power, and some others were all together. Power says, 'Look boys, what about a good damn slide down Prescott Hill?' St John's is not a flat city. Prescott Hill was about a mile from the top down to Water Street.

'How?' says another fellow.

Tom says, 'We'll go to Andy Carroll's forge and get one of them catamarans, then over to old Cashin's for two shutters.'

So we picked up a catamaran – they're exactly the

same as a sleigh, but with shafts standing up at one end
– then stole two window shutters from old Mr Cashin,
and tied them to the catamaran. We hauled to the top
of Prescott Hill and then started down with the eight of
us aboard. We had to cross three streets, Gower Street,
Duckworth Street, Water Street. Oh boy! It now began
going an awful rate, water running out of our eyes, and
if we'd have struck anything solid we'd have all been
killed. Well, at the bottom of the hill we jumped right
across Water Street, high in the air, and into Baldwin's
grocery store. We went right into and through the shop,
carrying the window sashes, glass, and everything with
us; knocking everything off the shelves, and nearly
killing two of the clerks, while we were scattered around
the shop bleeding like pigs. My people had to pay
Baldwin to put in the window again, and I got another
keelhauling.

Now came my final days in the Academy. Each desk
seated three boys, our slates on the desks in front of us.
There was a blackboard ran along the side of the
schoolroom for about twenty feet. We were allowed
home for dinner from one until two, and right after
dinner we would stand in front of the board in a
semicircle while the teacher, a Scotchman called Reid,
would explain something, an oak pointer in one hand,
a big lump of chalk in the other. One dinner-time I was
a few minutes late, and when I got to my desk, could
not see my slate. Reid called out what was the matter,

and to come up anyway. On my way I saw a big slate, but with no wooden fame around it, and grabbed it. When I reached the front I told him my slate had gone missing and he raised the pointer and rapped me on my left shoulder. I saw fire, made a swing, and BANG! went the slate which missed him by an inch or so but stuck in the blackboard about an inch and a half – the rest shattering and falling to the floor in pieces. He staggered back and fell up against the board, and I made for the hat-rack and out.

He wrote to my father for God's sake not to let me back. If he saw me come through the door again he would shake to pieces and faint. So that was the end of school.

2. Against my father's wishes I make two trips as 'Boy'– then begin my sea apprenticeship in the Liverpool ship, *Miranda* – after some adventures including drinking 'dead dog', I sail east and am arrested for stealing an idol – the captain lands a shark, but decides he'd be better throwing it back.

NEXT DOOR WAS Job Brothers, a Liverpool firm who owned the brig, *Mary*. The captain was Jersey man, Debrix, who I liked very much. I asked him to ship me as a 'Boy'. He asked my father, my mother came in on my behalf, and my father consented.

We sailed on 11 November, in a gale of nor'east wind. The bosun was an old devil named Jack Small, who always carried a strop. There was another boy shipped – Bob Waring, a Liverpool lad. All day it was 'Boy here!' and 'Boy there!' – and plenty of the strop if we were too long about it. At Pernambuco we took cotton and sugar for Liverpool, and had an awful passage to the Mersey. We then loaded for St John's, and running down the southeast Irish coast got a very heavy gust off the Tuskar Light, Wexford, and the captain carried sail longer than usual in order to clear the rocks, the most dangerous round that coast. Once we were clear the captain ordered three men out to stow sail on the jibboom, which sticks out a long way over the bows and the water. The ship took a sudden plunge and one of the men, George Stansbury, never came in, he was carried away. When this happened I was standing holding the fore-rigging near the pig-house. This had four iron bars across, so when the door was open the pigs could not get out. These bars were the thickness of my middle finger. That same sea that took George, took me from the rigging and drove my head right through those bars. It was ten minutes before anyone noticed, what with all the excitement around the jibboom. They tried to haul me out, but would have hauled my head off first. So they hooked a bar and bent it up. When they freed me, all the side of my head and ears were bleeding.

I will now tell a true story about George Stansbury. Back in St John's he had a wife and little girl. George went over at midnight, and about that time the child woke the mother by crying 'Daddy! Daddy!'– her hands stretched towards the door. The wife said she caught a glimpse of George – wet, and in his oilskins. She marked the date, and we arrived back eighteen days after. We sent for a priest to go and break the news to

her. But when she saw him enter the door she already
knew.

We arrived back the eighth day of March. I stayed
home a month or two, then signed as Boy for the West
Indies in a brigantine, *Alert*, Captain Prendergast,
called 'Nosey Dick Prender who murdered his crew.'
We went to Havana where yellow fever was raging:
every ship in the harbour had lost some crew, some had
lost all.

Prendergast had his wife aboard, and the night we
left they both went down with the fever while Maurice
Kane, a crew member, also took it. We were passing an
island called Inargua. We put in, just as Kane died
aboard. We took the captain and his wife ashore, and
got a negro woman to nurse them. Then we fumigated
the ship. In three or four days Prendergast and his wife
began to recover, and after eight we took them back on
board and set sail for home.

When we got back my father had been asked to stand
as Member for the East End of St John's. He laughed
and said, 'Hell! What do I know about politics? I know
more about fish and chips.' But my mother kept at him,
saying that people knew what they were doing. At least
she got legs under him, and he was returned with a big
majority as Minister of Agriculture and Mines.

In 1864, at fourteen, I began my official apprenticeship in a Liverpool ship, the *Miranda*, in which I
stayed about four years. Her general run was

triangular: Liverpool–St John's –the Brazils–Liverpool. The captain was Wakeham, from Brixham; a hard case. They all were, those old west of England men. You had to be a whole man before you dared to ship as an able seaman with people like Wakeham. If he gave you any job to do with rope or sail, and you could not do it, your wages would be cut to five shillings a month. The monthly pay then out of St John's was £3, or £3 10s. In England it was £2 10s to go East, fine weather voyages, and £3, or £3 5s, to go across the Atlantic. First mates received £6 or £7, and captains £10. In Newfoundland, the currency was pounds, shillings and pence when I started, but by the time I got to mate it was dollars and cents.

On the *Miranda* was another apprentice, John Warren. Here is our day. At six we would turn to with the crowd to wash the decks, fisting big holystones and squeegees, and brooms and rags. Then breakfast at eight bells – eight o'clock. After breakfast, Captain Wakeham would have the jollyboat taken off its skids and hung over the side. He would climb into the stern holding a piece of rope, then call to the mate, 'Where's them boys?' Warren and I would climb into the boat.

He would say, 'Warren, take that hand-lead and line, and coil it.' If Warren did not coil it right, he would get a cut of the captain's rope on his backside, with the words, 'Oh, you damned soldier!' If Warren got it right the captain would call, 'Heave!' Warren would let the line run out until the captain called 'Stop!' He would then say, 'What have you got?'

Warren would consult the line, then bawl out in a singing way, 'By the deep, twelve!' Or, perhaps, 'A quarter less twelve!' Or, 'By the mark, thirteen!' Or, 'And a half, thirteen!'

You see, on a ship, we have two leads. The 'deep-sea lead', and the 'hand-lead'. The deep-sea lead-line is marked every five fathoms up to 120, or 130, fathoms. The hand-lead, however, is smaller, and only used going in and out of harbour, and is marked up to twenty fathoms.

After Warren had had his cuts on his hindquarters, he would pass the line to me. It would not be long before I would sample the rope, and eventually both of us would be dismissed with 'Oh, you lubbers! Get to hell, for'd, you pair of greenhorns!' and the man at the wheel grinning away at us.

The mate would then set me cleaning brasswork around the wheel, and on the hoops of the buckets. Warren would go below, being on the second mate's watch – I was in the mate's. There is always one watch below – one on deck – four hours about. All except when it's 'All hands', in a storm or other emergency. But so you don't have the same watch on deck all the time they split the evening watch – the 4pm to 8pm watch – into two watches of two hours each; these are called the dog-watches.

We apprentices lived in a forecabin next to the captain's cabin, but with its own door. With us lived the sailmaker and carpenter. On Sunday we four of us had to dress in our best, and go to dinner in the cabin with the captain and mates, always a good blow-out, with plum pudding with plenty of currants and raisins. This was eagerly looked forward to, as at other times we ate as the crew did: in them days, very bad. Salt beef and duff one day, pea soup and pork the next – through seven days; on Saturday boiled rice, called 'sky-blue' – no sugar or anything. Everything weighed out; one pound of sugar per week. You never saw a bit of butter all trip, though they had it in the cabin. But never any soft bread either in the fo'c'sle or the cabin. The officers would have white pilot biscuits, but in the fo'c'sle it was Liverpool pantiles. These were dark – a mixture of flour, oatmeal and ground-up straw. You couldn't bite them with your teeth. You had to take them on deck and break them with an iron belaying pin. Breakfast was pantiles plus black coffee with no milk. Tea in the evening was the same, unless you saved a bit of pork from dinner. But what we got was little enough without keeping some of it back for tea. So our weekly meal in the cabin, as apprentices, was much looked forward to.

There is a story I want to tell you about a later trip and one of those Sunday meals in the cabin. We had arrived in St John's from Liverpool in November. The day after we arrived, the carpenter, Legg, bought a fine

Newfoundland pup. This pup would be around the decks all day, and when we finished our meals, Legg would give the dog our leftovers; in port we had plenty as we could buy stuff ashore. We were working day and night discharging and loading, and the night before she sailed everyone, as usual, was very busy. After tea, Legg called his pup, but it wasn't to be found. Legg blamed some of the shore labourers for stealing him, kicking up a terrible fuss. Fuss or not the dog wasn't found, and we sailed for Brazil with our usual cargo, salted codfish in barrels.

We were about thirty days getting to the equator. It was so hot the pitch was bubbling in the seams. That Sunday, as usual, Warren and I were dining in the cabin. After a few mouthfuls, the captain, Wakeham, took the big water jug and poured himself a glass. He took a mouthful, looked hard at the glass, then called in the steward from the pantry. He holds up the glass.

'There's hairs in this,' he says. 'Was the jug washed before you pumped water into it?'

'Yes, sir,' replies the steward, 'washed well.'

'Well, do it again and bring another jugful.'

The steward took it out on deck to the tank pump, refilled it, brought it back down. The captain filled a fresh glass and held it to the light. It was full of lots of black hairs, about an inch and a half long.

The mate, Dingle, suddenly jumped to his feet. 'Good God! That's where the dog went!'

You should have seen it. The carpenter, Legg, almost fainted. The captain began abusing him fit to beat the band. The mate and I, who had had some water from the first filling, ran up to the rail and almost vomited our insides out. I was tasting dead dog for a week. On ships, the carpenter is always responsible for the water. It seems, the day before sailing, Legg was filling the water tank in the dark. He had the manhole cover off, with a hose running in water from the shore. He went to his carpenter's shop to get some white lead to put round the tank flange to make the seal. The dog must have jumped up onto the flange and fallen in. Legg came back, and screwed on the cover in the dark. The dog had now been in the tank thirty days – the tank that contained all our fresh water. We were still four days from Pernambuco, and it was as hot as Hades. We had to drink it, and no one could do so without vomiting. I used to pick the hairs out, and then add vinegar, that way I did not get the taste of dog. The carpenter seemed ready to jump overboard or commit suicide.

At Pernambuco Warren and I had to clean out the tank. When we got to the bottom there was the dog, whitish blue, and completely hairless. We shovelled him into a big bucket, and the men hoisted him up and dumped him over the side.

On the *Miranda*, all the crew of fourteen, but two, was under twenty-five. Joe Banks was our leader, another Liverpool boy. There was nothing too hot for Joe to hold, too heavy to lift. We had to follow him when and wherever, or pay a forfeit. He would start by going up the leech, the edge of the foresail, then up the topsail, the topgallant and royal; then across between the masts on one of the stays, then back to the foremast again. Old Wakeham would enjoy it as much as we did

One of the older men was Sweeney – my 'fancy man'. That is, the able seaman who showed me how to splice, and knot, and graft. He knew everything good and bad. One night, running from the Brazils to Liverpool, he says to me, 'Billy, I want you to get me a little sugar and butter out of the pantry. They'll never miss it.'

On the port side of where we lived in the forecabin was a square hole in the bulkhead with a slider, known as a 'nor'wester'. From this you could get into the mate Dingle's, room, with the pantry right opposite. I waited till Dingle was on deck, then crawled through the slider wearing a big shirt, and a belt round my waist. Into the shirt, in bags, I put three or four pounds of sugar, and wrapped the same amount of butter in a big sheet of paper. I packed the space around with cabin biscuit, then smuggled the lot forward to Sweeney. Of course, others got to know, and one soon told the mate, because, about a week after, on the job again, I was just struggling back through the nor'wester when Dingle grabbed me by the seat of my pants. I began to cry as Dingle called for the captain. Wakeham came in, and

Dingle hauled up my shirt, and out dropped the sugar, butter, and all.

The captain looked at me. 'You damned young thief! Who was that for?'

I said, 'For myself!'

At this he kicked and cuffed me up the stairs, and told me I would be tried the next morning At eight next day I was piped aft, and the captain said, 'Now, Billy. Either tell me who put you up to it, or you're in irons till we reach Liverpool – and then go to jail. So who was it?'

Again I said, 'It was for myself, sir!'

Then he got nice, and smiled, and said, 'I know it's someone for'd. But I like you. So tell me and I'll forgive you.'

Again I said nothing, and he looked hard and said, 'All right. But I like you all the same – but, mind, don't try it again!' The captain was a rough old fellow, but all right, and good-hearted.

I spoke to Joe Banks and we decided to play a trick on Dingle. When you load with green new sugar, there is this awful smell in the cabin from the cargo steam coming up from the hold. So Dingle would sleep on deck under the lifeboat, which is always turned bottom-up, on blocks, on top of the fo'c'sle house. It was this cargo smell which gave us the idea. One night, when Dingle dropped off to sleep, Banks went up and got down one of Dingle's boots. I won't tell you what we put in it – nothing very nice. At one bell, quarter to four in the morning, I went up to call Dingle. I finally roused him and you could have heard him coughing, spitting and groaning back in Pernambuco. We heard him haul on one boot, and stamp it on the deck. Nothing yet. Then we heard him putting on the other boot and stamping it. Oh boy! He came tumbling down the ladder, holding and shaking his boot, and swearing like a trooper as he pointed off towards the cabin, his stocking leaving a telltale track on the deck.

Wakeham was at first a bit slow, being frightened out of his sleep with the mate crying, 'Captain, look what they did to my boot!' Then the captain got the smell from the boot and stocking. He rushed across the cabin, and grabbed the mate.

'Damn you! How dare you come in here with that damned stinking boot!' That was all the consolation the mate got that night.

Next morning all hands were drummed to quarters. The captain stood on the break of the poop, Dingle alongside him. Dingle's face had murder written in it; the captain could hardly keep his straight.

The captain began, 'Now then! Which of you did this dirty deed on the mate? Was it you, Banks?'

'No, sir.'

'Barnes?'

'No, sir.'

The mate could keep quiet no longer, 'Captain, I believe it was Banks!'

47

'Well, Banks?' asked Wakeham.

'I believe it was himself, sir,' said Joe, thoughtful-like, 'to get us into trouble.'

The captain, about to explode with laughter, said, 'That's enough. Go for'd now. But you will all pay for it before Liverpool,' the captain enjoying the joke as much as we did.

That was a trip I'll never forget: calms and light winds, so we were seventy-five days getting to within three hundred miles of Queenstown – and then a calm that had been there for about a month. Ships congregated from all ends of the world; some a year out, some two years that had barnacles and conches and grasses on their bottoms; some it would take half a gale to move them. The *Miranda*, though it was wooden built, was bottom coppered, and so we wormed along, about a quarter of a mile an hour. As we passed, ship after ship sent boats saying they were starving. We ourselves were now out seventy-five days, living just on rice, and two small dippers of water per day per man. All we could give them was our cargo – sugar. Some ships would get three bags, some four or five according to their size, and the number of crew. Wakeham said he would not see them starve, and someone would pay for it. After about a week, steamers were sent out loaded with provisions. We got into Queenstown looking like skeletons.

After week we were ordered to Bristol then to St John's in late November when a gale, a hurricane, started in on us. A sea struck us about noon, which smashed the two boats on top of the fo'c'sle, and stove in part of the starboard side, filling the fo'c'sle and washing half the watch below out of their bunks. Every movable thing on deck went overboard, the cook eventually being picked up aft against the break of the poop. The wind shifted and reshifted – it was heartbreaking. At last we got to the Newfoundland Banks, three hundred miles from St John's. And now came snow and frost. You went aloft to bend sail but, of course, you couldn't work with your mitts on. They would stick to the rigging and your hand would pull out, and you'd fall and kill yourself, or go overboard. We were halfway across the Banks when a terrible sea took away the binnacle and compass, smashed the cabin skylight, and filled the cabin with water. All the stanchions and the bulwarks from the starboard side went, together with the starboard anchor. Two men went overboard, plus the man at the wheel who went with the compass and binnacle. I escaped as I was watch below at the time. And now came a nice fair wind from the nor'west and we got to St John's three days after. It seemed we had left Bristol a year previous. It was all over the papers, and my father asked how I liked the sea now. 'I like it fine,' I told him. He said no more.

My last trip on the *Miranda* we ran from St John's to Rio, then charted for Liverpool. We were a month there, and had a great time going round with apprentices from other ships. There was a big public house right opposite the dock and about forty or fifty of us boys used to meet of an evening to play games. Poor Captain Smith of the *Titanic* was an apprentice at that time, and I was well acquainted with him, we would take walks together. He was a nice fellow as a boy.

I was four years running back and forwards to Liverpool. It was during this time I began to learn about sailors properly, and things like shanghaiing, boarding houses, and girls. And from there I made my first trips out east.

Before we leave the *Miranda*, I'll tell you what happened on one of those long trips out east. We loaded for Singapore, discharged, then loaded back for Liverpool. Before we sailed Warren and I were ashore walking around and came to an estate owned by one of those mandarins, so rich they don't know what money they have. They have these gods they worship – little wooden gods painted up beautiful in blue jackets and red caps, three or four feet high, standing round their gardens. Well, we stood looking through the gates at this god and I'll tell you what, we both fell in love with it. Of course we were still both children – about fifteen.

Warren says, 'We'll come back after dark. If we can get it back to Liverpool we can sell it to some big bug, any money we like to ask.'

So that night we drew lots, Warren went in and passed it over the fence, and we began carrying it back to the ship, fore and aft, with my coat over its body, and Warren's waistcoat over its head. Now, the police there wear regular army coats, and carry a gun with a fixed bayonet. One saw us, ripped off my coat, and caught sight of the god. He trembled all over as if he believed he would be struck dead, walked about ten foot away, pointed his gun, and it was 'left, right' to jail.

At the jail they were almost too terrified to handle the thing, but hauled it away somehow and shoved us in a cell. We began to cry as some of them were nasty devils – peering though the door with their hands round their necks to let us know we'd be hung. Warren cried even louder.

'Aw,' said I, 'Wait until we get it!' I talked Warren round, and by and by we both fell asleep.

Next morning we had breakfast and were booked – names, ship, captain – then shoved back in the cell.

About ten, Captain Wakeham comes in. 'You damn scoundrels,' he says. 'You'll hang!' Warren began to cry again. 'You'll cry when you get that rope round your neck,' Wakeham told him, then went away.

In half an hour the soldiers came and took us to court. Here we saw the captain, the ship's agent, the consignees, the consul, and two or three other English gentlemen. There was an Indian could speak English as well as we could, and he was our lawyer. We stood in front of the judge, the captain and the rest of our crowd ranged alongside.

The lawyer says, 'Judge, of course they were caught stealing a god – they just didn't know it was a god. They are only boys – look at them! They saw its bright colours – and like any baby likes a doll, picked it up to bring home. These boys don't know the religion here, judge. They're just young apprentices.'

The judge, who could speak good English as well, says, 'They knew they were stealing – and that stealing is a crime.'

Now in came the big mandarin who owned the idol, frothing at the mouth, dancing up and down, and talking to the judge in his own language. Wouldn't have been as excited, I don't think, if he heard his wife and children were dead. And now everyone on both sides began to fume, but I suppose the judge didn't want to fall out with the English, and so fined us both twenty dollars. The captain paid, and they let us go, but, by God, when we got back aboard Wakeham gave us such a booting and clouting I can feel it now.

The last thing that happened was on the way back to Liverpool. We'd just crossed the Line back into the North Atlantic, and saw a big shark swimming after the ship. Immediately Wakeham called out to the carpenter, 'Bring the shark hook and a piece of pork!' A shark hook is about the size of your middle finger, with a barb on its tip, and a rope spliced into it about twenty fathoms long.

Mister Shark must have been right hungry, for, no

DISCOVER MORE ABOUT MARITIME HISTORY

Seaforth Publishing is a maritime imprint of Pen & Sword Books, which has over 1500 titles in print covering all aspects of military history on land, sea and air. If you would like to receive more information and special offers on your preferred interests from time to time, along with our standard catalogue, please indicate your areas of interest below and return this card (no stamp required in the UK). Alternatively, register online at www.seaforthpublishing.com. Thank you.

PLEASE NOTE: We do not sell data information to any third party companies.

Mr/Mrs/Ms/Other............... Name..

Address...

.... Postcode............................

Email address..

If you wish to receive our email newsletter, please tick here ☐

PLEASE SELECT YOUR AREAS OF INTEREST

Naval - The Wooden Walls ☐	The Merchant Marine ☐		
Naval - Iron & Steel Navies ☐	Ship Modelling ☐		
Sail & Traditional Craft ☐	General Maritime ☐	ALL ☐	

Website: www.seaforthpublishing.com • Email: info@seaforthpublishing.com
Telephone: 01226 734555 • Fax: 01226 734438

2

Seaforth Publishing
FREEPOST SF5
47 Church Street
BARNSLEY
South Yorkshire
S70 2BR

sooner we put it over than he shot up and took it all down. It took five or six of us to haul him under the stern, but now the problem was how to get him aboard. Sometimes he would jump up, sometimes crook himself, sometimes swing his tail. Anyway, we finally got his nose hauled up to the stern rail, then a running bowline around his middle and a hook in the tackle, and now we had him swinging. Then we hauled him six feet above the ship's rail, pulled him aboard by the shark hook, and dropped him on the deck. He was a monster – fifteen feet long. Oh boy! Now he began to work his tail. One blow broke all the thick plate glass in the skylights and knocked out the sashes. Then he began working towards the beautiful mahogany, brass-bound, steering wheel – the man on the wheel, after taking one look, clearing out at the run just before Mr Shark swung and broke it all up. The main braces were stacked neatly on the deck in Flemish coils, but he was soon entwined and entwisted in them.

Old Wakeham was now roaring, 'Carpenter! Carpenter! Get your axe and cut off his tail!'

The carpenter ran forward for his axe, then jumped around waiting his chance at a cut. At last he took a swing, missed altogether, and gouged a deep gash through the deck and into the cabin. Two more times he did the same, and with each cut into his teakwood deck, the captain groaned as if dying. The fourth time he swung, the carpenter hit about four feet from the end of the tail and nearly cut it through. Now the fish was still squirming, but quieter. But now, each time he gave another 'quish' of his tail – you'd think we'd just come out after Trafalgar with the amount of blood flying everywhere. He was also still ensnared in the ropes which we could not get from him, for if he caught your leg with one of his snaps it was off. We had to cut through all the ropes and braces to haul him from the poop to the main deck, and now the captain began yelling, 'Get the damn thing overboard! You hear me!' So we reversed proceedings and finally got him over the side and cut him adrift. He swam off leaving a streak of blood behind, but coasting away if nothing else had ever happened. Old Wakeham was nearly crying.

The rest of the passage the carpenter spent repairing the skylight and cursing sharks with every breath. One day a fellow sang out, 'Shark on the port bow!' The carpenter jumped as if shot.

When we reached Liverpool they had to let two long planks into the deck. But there were no more sharks for Captain Wakeham after that – not ever.

3. Before the mast in the *Jane* – race of the 'fish-boxes' – I take fever at Bahia – hospitalised I almost die of starvation but escape – the men become delirious howling and baying about the decks leaving four of us to work the ship. The steward deliberately swallows a sovereign – we finally make New York – at the quarantine station the doctor is told that one of our crew who is still bright orange with fever is 'sun-scorched'.

AFTER LEAVING THE *Miranda*, I shipped before the mast in the *Jane* – a Newfoundland 'fish-box'. Those days, the 1860s, the hardest driven ships afloat were the fish-boxes and the China tea clippers – because both had to run for market. With the fish-boxes, when the season opened, the first ship down to Pernambuco would get the best prices. There were always heavy bets on this – up to £500 English money. As well, the first captain down would get fifty dollars, the profit off fifty drums of fish, and a new beaver hat. That year it was understood the contest would be between the *Jane* and the *Meteor*. The *Jane* was a Greenock brig, Captain McNeil. A good man but liked his whisky too well; perhaps, like many, it gave him the courage to carry sail under strong winds. Both ships set off, and after a week at sea we were making about ten miles an hour, the captain on deck all day except when he would go below to 'freshen the nip' as sailors say.

He'd come up smoking his pipe, look aloft and say, 'Go it, *Jane*! – Go it, old girl!' Then it started to blow up, and about 11pm the topgallant sheet carried away, and before we could get the sail clewed up it was in ribbons. The mate asked McNeil if he was thinking of taking off any sail.

'Not a damned rag,' says McNeil. 'Go to hell! Get another sail bent!'

Next to go was the jibboom, and with it the three jibs. The mate asked if the captain would lay the *Jane*'s head off a couple of points, 'To give her a chance'.

'Not a damned point!'

Cursing and swearing, we spent all night clearing wreckage, up to our waists in water, and not knowing when any of us might be washed overboard. This went on for five days, by which time we were nearly at the equator, still no sign of the *Meteor*. I must tell you all ships going south for the Brazils have to cross the Line at pretty well the same latitude. So one morning came the cry, 'Ship on the star'bd bow!' – the *Meteor*, their captain, Smith, having lost his fore topgallant mast in the same storm.

And now the wind dropped completely, and we had three or four hundred miles of calms to work through before picking up the southeast trades. We would get the odd 'cat's-paw' – now one side, now the other, all hands swearing and cursing, for in the doldrums the sailors never stop hauling and bracing. This went on till we sighted Olinda Point about four miles away, itself about four miles from Pernambuco. The *Meteor* was about five miles astern of us.

It fell calm again, and McNeil, pacing the deck, and swearing like a trooper, said to the mate, 'We can't let them beat us. Put over the jollyboat – two drums of fish in her. We'll row to the guard ship in Pernambuco harbour, let the merchants see what we have, and call a quick sale!'

This meant a row, under a blazing sun, of eight miles. The jollyboat would have four oars; I would be one. Now, every morning on that ship I would draw up a bucket of saltwater and pour it over my head, the brine drying in my hair. Once we began rowing hard, I began to perspire, so much so that the salt ran down out of my hair into my eyes. I was in great pain, the pickle burning my eyes, and me rubbing them. By the time we reached the guard ship I could hardly see.

Now the captain called for the agent, who notified the

buyers. They rushed offshore to look in the specimen drums, and the whole cargo, five thousand drums, was knocked down at 27 *milreas* a drum. The *milreas* at that time was worth about one shilling and sixpence, which made about £2 English a drum, £10,000 English all told. Captain McNeil not only got his £50, his profit on the first fifty barrels, and a new beaver hat, but also an extra twenty sovereigns from the consignee as a gratuity. About 2pm, under a nice breeze, in came the *Meteor*. When Captain Smith heard what our captain had done he nearly went mad.

Now I went for officer. I joined old Matty Dunn – the 'King of Ugly' – in the *Queen of Beauty* as second mate, then went mate in the *Island Lass* in 1871 at the age of twenty.

I then heard the *Rival*, Captain Branscombe, was loading for Brazil while her mate, Morris, was going to Halifax to be examined for captain, and if I liked I could take his place. At that time the yellow fever was very bad in the Brazils; a lot of men had died and I believed Morris was frightened to go, making sitting the examination his excuse.

I decided I'd ship, and we sailed for Pernambuco and had a good passage of thirty-five days. We were ordered onto Bahia, where we arrived five days later. Here the fever was even worse, but we began to discharge. In those days, the crew, rather than dock labourers, discharged the cargoes. About noon on the first day, the man on the starboard winch gave out. Branscombe was onshore, but had ordered me, if anyone got sick, to hoist the yellow (fever) flag at once. I did, and the hospital boat came alongside and took the winchman away. The next day the same, and the next. The hospital boat was busy all day long from one ship to another. We got the cargo out, and I was just mixing a pot of paint on deck when I felt awful sick. I went aft and sat on the fore-end of the cabin-house. I felt what others had told me – pains in the back of the neck, and calves of the legs, cold chills, perspiration, pulse racing, temples throbbing. The captain came on board, looked at my tongue, felt my pulse, and shipped me off to hospital.

Branscombe was a fine fellow, coming to see us every day. He told me that I'd gone for him once while I was delirious, saying he'd cut me out with my girl. If I was delirious it was with starvation, because that was the method at that hospital – no feeding, in order to kill the fever. By the time I'd been there a week I would have eaten a dead horse; a dead man as long as he was cooked.

While I was there about forty different sailors died. In the end bed, next to mine, was a fine young man, mate of a French barque. He'd been bad, too, but seemed to be getting better. We became great chums and would sit on the verandah, and he'd play the accordion and I'd sing; I used to sing very well.

The interpreter at the hospital had been an officer in

the army during the Paraguayan war, and had two beautiful daughters. The best-looking was head over heels in love with the French mate, anybody could see it. One Sunday morning we were all sitting there talking and playing, when all at once he took bad. It was about ten o'clock.

I told him to go and lie down. 'You're doing too much,' I said, 'and we're starved to death.' He went in. I sat for an hour or two trying to play the accordion. I didn't know how then, though since I've learned.

A porter came out, and I says, 'Where's my friend?'

'Oh. Very bad. I tink he die.'

I went in and he wasn't dead, but didn't know me. I sat outside for a time, then went for a walk round the garden. There was a large tent I hadn't been in before. I opened the door and it was piled up, tier after tier, with coffins. They were a lead colour. I didn't want to look long, I can tell ye, so I went and laid on my bed. About four I saw the porters running in and out.

'What now?' I said.

'Oh,' says one of them, 'Friend die. He go. Die!'

Now I did feel sick. Good God! I'd never had such a turn. I saw them go in with a coffin, and in about half an hour they brought him out and took him round the end of the hospital. I followed, and they loaded him in a hearse, gave the horse a crack, and away it went full gallop up the road. No funeral. That was the end of the French second mate. He'd had 'the black vomit', a second relapse. I cried for him that night as if my own brother had died.

Now I decided I was leaving the hospital. I was calling for food all the time but, 'No! No!' said the doctor. 'No food.'

'Then I want to go,' said I. 'Because if I am dying – it's of hunger!'

'No! No! No!' to that as well.

Next morning I got my walking stick and made my way about a hundred and fifty yards to the bottom of the garden where I couldn't be seen. It was a beautiful garden – all full of trees. Its wall was about ten feet high. I threw my stick over, got on top, lowered myself the length of my arms, and dropped. Usually I would have landed on my feet, but being a bit weak I fell backwards. Once up, I pointed my nose towards town and set off. I was wearing hospital rig: a white calico skull cap, a long white gown, and slippers. The slippers had no heels and kept coming off. The city was about three miles away and at about eleven the sun began to blaze, the sand hot as hell under my feet. Eventually I got off the beach and onto the streets, everyone staring and keeping about ten feet clear of me. I was still yellow in the face, and they thought I was insane, or at the point of death. I was pretty tired myself by then. I made for Wilson's, the ships' chandlers. I went in and bolted the door behind me. George Wilson himself was behind the counter – also present were a lot of captains as

Wilson had some nice card and billiard tables, and a nice little back parlour.

'Good God,' says Wilson. 'Is that you, Mr Barnes? Did they send you out of hospital like that?'

'I'd had enough. So I got over the wall and walked along the beach.'

'There'll be murder over this,' said Wilson. At this all the other captains jumped to their feet. One looked at his watch – somewhere he needed to be. Another had some other place to go. Before you could say 'knife' there wasn't a man left at those tables. Wilson put me in the back parlour and sent for Branscombe. I looked at him.

'I was starving to death,' I told him.

'They'll be after you.'

'There's a lot of old clothes in a slop chest,' says Wilson. We went in the back room and I pulled up the nightshirt that was on me and tied it round my waist. Then, from the slop-chest, I pulled out an old reefing jacket, a cap, some boots and an old pair of pants, all belonging to a sailor who was dead.

'Better get him on board before they come looking,' says Wilson to Branscombe.

'I'll kill them if they try and put me back in there,' says I. The captain brought me to the landing-slip, took out some money, called a boat.

'Here,' he says. 'This is the mate of the *Rival*. Put him aboard.'

They rowed me out, and I got up the ladder and headed straight to the galley. Old Scully, the cook, looked at me. I didn't say a word but headed for the pantry. There was a big tureen of soup. Not much had gone because with that sort of weather you don't eat much. I lifted that tureen to my mouth and drank all there was. Then I looked in the locker and saw a lot of cold potatoes, and cabbage, and some fresh beets. I went for them like a dog: no knife or fork, like a dog. God! I had good teeth in them days! And when there was no more I went out on deck and laid down as ill again as I ever was.

The captain came aboard. 'What's the matter?'

'I'm sick again.'

'Look. The doctor and interpreter came roaring into Wilson's after you left. I greased their palms – but agreed to take you ashore again if you had a relapse, and that's what you've got now.'

While he was talking I fell asleep. When I woke in the middle of the night I was all right. I had a smoke, went back to sleep, and in the morning was as good as ever I was. And that was the end of me and the fever.

But that night, the night we left, a stowaway, a little boy called Jimmy Cahill laid down, and one look told us it was the fever. Then one day after another the rest who had so far made it – all the fo'c'sle crowd – all lay down. Now it was the captain, myself, the second mate, Jimmy Kane, and the steward, Ned Ellis. The weather turned fine so there wasn't much sail handling, so the three of us took turns pumping and steering, while the steward, Ned Ellis, was in the galley.

But now Ned took it, and was down on his cabin floor in deliriums, talking nonsense, while the fo'c'sle hands all became delirious as well. To kill the fever we wouldn't give them much to eat or drink, like at the hospital, and they were bawling all the time for food and water. They'd come out the foc's'le on their hands and knees, like dogs, and crawl for the water cask.

I'd come down from the quarterdeck, yelling, 'Clear away from that cask or I'll kill you!' They would look at me as if I was going to go for them with an axe, then crawl back to the fo'c'sle.

Every morning, soon as I had my breakfast, not before, I'd take a bucket of water and a big Turks Island sponge and go forward, and take them out one by one, and swab them from head to heels. When they were out of their senses, you see, they'd neglect themselves. It was a hell of a job. The hot steam from the hot water on their hot bodies would throw off this terrible stench into my face. Sometimes they used to complain, ask what I was doing.

I'd say, 'Shut up or I'll kill you!' One night two of them got to fighting and the captain sent me down. When I got there, there were two of them, half-naked, rolling round, all the others shouting 'Murder!' One stated the other was killing him with a knife, except there was no knife there. All the time the others were continually howling. It was worse than any lunatic asylum.

The captain now took over the cooking, while Kane and I did the ship's work. Kane and I used to have to approach the delirious cook, Ned Ellis, to get anything the captain might want for the pot. One morning Kane went down for something, then jumped up pretty quick to the skylight where I'm talking to the captain.

'The cook has a sovereign in his mouth!' says Kane.

'Didn't you try to take it out?' says Branscombe. 'Next thing he'll swallow it.'

'And get my fingers bit off?' says Kane. 'Some fool I'd be.'

Branscombe swung round to me, 'Mr Barnes. Go down will you?'

Ned Ellis, tailor by trade, was lying on the floor when I got down, grinning at a sovereign in the palm of his hand. He must have had it hidden it away somewhere, and, gripped by fever, now thought someone might come looking for it. When he saw me, he immediately whipped it into his mouth. I ran up and shoved my fingers in, and ran them round, but it was gone. He'd swallowed it. I had a second try, and, as Kane mentioned, he damn near bit my finger off. I shook my fist at him and went back aloft.

'He's swallowed it,' I said.

'My God,' says the captain, 'I wonder will he pass it?'

Then turned to Kane, 'Jim,' he said, 'It will be your job to watch if he passes it.'

'Be damned to that,' says Kane, a surly old fellow who never regarded how he spoke to anyone.

'You've got to,' says the captain. 'Get a belaying pin to churn it up and see what's there.'

Kane stomped off while I was killing myself laughing on the skylight. But now Branscombe told me to watch Kane watching the steward. And we did, though Kane didn't try very hard. But we never found the sovereign. Ellis got over the fever, but died about a year later anyway. Both Branscombe and I believed it was because the sovereign got stuck in him somewhere.

Now all hands started to recover except two that died, but now Branscombe wouldn't eat any bread because Ellis mixed the dough with his hands, and so began living off biscuits and coffee. We'd two cocks and fifteen good laying hens on board, and Branscombe told Ellis to kill them and make a good broth to help the men recover their strength, as he was afraid they would not pass the quarantine doctor in New York, and the ship would be held up and the owners blame the captain. We finally made New York, with Branscombe himself now in a fever, but only because the men still looked so sickly.

He said to them, 'Now, boys. We'll be seeing the doctor off Staten Island. So all look cheerful and talk a lot, because, if you don't, we're going into quarantine for thirty days.'

We anchored about eight that night. It was dark, and the crew lined up and the doctor came along and looked at them. I was shivering myself at the thought of being stuck out there another thirty days. Well, the doctor made one fellow hold out his tongue – another his hand while he felt his pulse – and then reached one fellow who was a bright orange colour.

He turned to Branscombe. 'Captain,' he says, 'This man is awful yellow-looking. Has there been any sickness lately?'

'Well, doctor,' says the captain, 'where we've been this last month. Well, if you had the sun right overhead, you'd be the same yourself. The truth is this man is "scorched".'

The doctor looked, then smiled, then said, 'Yes, I suppose so.' He was suspicious. But it was dark, and if he stopped the ship, and the captain called for another doctor at daylight who passed us – well, this first doctor might feel he'd made a fool of himself. So he gave the nod and we got up to Governor's Island and next day we towed up to Prentice's Wharf, Brooklyn, and started to work cargo. And that was the end of the yellow fever on the *Rival*.

4. 1873–1875. I meet Elma – first love
– sail with Captain Doderidge for
Greenock – Doderidge is lost
overboard and I am made captain at
Greenock but cannot sail because I
have no certificate – I put another
captain in the ship which I can do
because I am captain, though I cannot
sail as captain – travel home
passenger.

I WAS A captain before I was captain – here's how it
happened. Hugh Doderidge came to St John's from New
Richmond in a vessel owned by his father, his brothers,
and himself. Doderidge, who was big and heavy, only
had one hand he could use. He'd had a spree in the
country with seven or eight pals, and coming home they
were all beswacked, and the carriage tumbled at a
corner, and when Doderidge got up his right arm was
crippled. The doctors made a bad job of it, and he
ended with his hand all bent up, his fingers touching
his wrist. All he could do was swing it and make a hook
of it. I liked Doderidge a lot.

Now Doderidge lost his ship without any insurance, so his brother-in-law, Mr Campbell, who was pretty wealthy, built the brig *Elma* for him, just to give Doderidge a living. The ship was named after Campbell's niece, Elma, who lived with him, her mother having died some years previous.

I met Doderidge in the street one day and he said, 'Come into Lasher's with me,' a bar that that was there at the time. We talked about this and that, and he says, 'Look, Barnes. My mate has cleared off – he was no good anyway. Will you ship mate with me? You're doing nothing, are you?'

'No,' I says. Then, 'I'll go.'

It was summer, and in summer Doderidge would run timber and shingles between New Richmond and St John's – although in winter he always favoured the Mediterranean or Caribbean. So we ran up to New Richmond where he brought me ashore and introduced me to his family. Every night there would be a party or 'cloth-thickening'. I'll tell you about cloth-thickening. It would start about five in the evening – a crowd of young men and girls. In a barn they'd have a long table about four feet wide, with a rim all around of about two and a half inches. All the young people would get round the table and pour water onto it, to about half way up the rim. Then they'd bring out bars of soap they'd cut into chunks. Then all hands would work away until they got a good lather. Then they'd bring in a roll of cloth and unroll it along the table – shoving it back and forwards towards each other. The lather would fly in your face and get in your eyes. The fellows opposite the girls they'd fancy would shove it up into their faces, and the girls would get handfuls of suds and throw them back. After about an hour, they'd take the cloth off and wash the table down – then fill it with clean water and get the heaviest of the soap out of the cloth. Then they'd roll it and let it shrink during the night. Then afterwards, there would be a dance. It was all great fun.

One Saturday, Doderidge says, 'Come ashore and have dinner with me and the wife.'

'All right,' says I.

'We'll go to church first,' he said.

I think it was called the Scotch kirk, and when we came out Mr Campbell, the brother-in-law who built the *Elma*, was there with the niece, Elma, both standing near Campbell's little wagon. I was twenty-three now and she was two or three years younger, and a nice-looking girl.

Doderidge introduced me, and, after we'd stood talking a bit, Campbell said, 'Well, we must be getting home. Come on, Barnes. Come over and have dinner. Jump in the wagon with Elma and me.'

Doderidge winked at me, 'Go on,' he said.

At the carriage I was introduced to Elma and shook hands, and Campbell put the pair of us in the back seat. We got across the bay to the house and had dinner.

Afterwards he said 'Barnes, I always like a good nap after my dinner.' So he called for Elma who was out in the hall and told her to bring the wagon and take me for a drive. I said nothing; I was awful shy in them days – still am. Anyways, we went out to get the horse. I knew as much about horses as a horse does about ships. I backed him into the shafts to help get the shackling on him. I saw what I came to learn were called 'traces'.

I said to Elma, 'Shall I haul these back-ropes up tight?' She said, 'Them are traces.'

I told her I called them back-ropes because they come from the back of the horse. Elma laughed fit to kill herself. We got into the carriage and drove round until about half past five, when we got back for tea. After we'd eaten Elma played the piano and sang for me. And I sang too. 'Juanita' and 'By The Sad Sea Waves' – all of them. At eight I said I had to go to get back on the ship, that it would be ten before I made it, and I had to be up at six to turn the men to.

'All right,' says Campbell, 'But don't be a stranger. Come over whenever you like.' Elma came down to the wicket gate with me and we chatted for a bit and I left.

Next day Doderidge came aboard and asked me how I got on. I said Campbell and I had an enjoyable chat.

'He's like that,' said Doderidge. 'Talk the sleeve out of a coat.' After this Elma and I used to write to one another, and then I picked up with the girl I married, and, of course, forgot about Elma.

Winter came on, and Doderidge began to think of chartering for warm weather: the West Indies, Spain, or Portugal. That year there weren't too many boats loading for the Brazils, many having lost their crews to the fever so freights were very high. Now, the *Elma* would carry five thousand drums of fish and Doderidge was offered four shillings a drum for Pernambuco, £1,000 in all. But Doderidge, though big, was faint-hearted, and awful scared of yellow fever. So he refused.

As it is only once in a Dutch moon you get a freight like that, I said to him, 'Give me charge of the ship for this trip, and you can stay home.'

He says back to me, 'I don't know but I will.'

But there was a Scotch house there, James and William Stuart, and they had a cargo for Greenock: sea-oil in casks, and sealskins, in bulk, in salt, and a couple of thousand quintals of codfish. So they chartered Doderidge for a lump sum – £520 for all they could get into her. And he took it. I was vexed, but, of course, I stayed with him, and we started to load for Greenock. Now, as I said, it was 'all they could get into her', and the Stuarts, between the casks of oil jammed sealskins rolled in bundles. By the time they finished the ship was as deep as a sand barge, and us having to take her across the North Atlantic in winter. That was in January 1875 and just before we sailed my mother died, and Doderidge delayed the vessel for two days so I could see her buried.

We left St John's 10am on 11 January. There was eleven men all told on the *Elma*, all 'farmers'. 'Farmers' is what is called sailors who sign and can't do their jobs. Sometimes they're called 'soldiers' or 'sojers'. But these mainly were real farmers. You see, on our last run up to Richmond, the crew paid off and took the ferry for Merimachia where they got a boat across the Atlantic – they were old country, most of them. So when Doderidge was ready there were no sailors. Now these farmers, their hay was in, harvesting was over, and the potatoes and everything could be left to the women. So they thought they'd come to earn plenty of money – Doderidge paid good wages – and spend the winter on a pleasure trip. One of them was Heck Campbell, old Doderidge's nephew: big, soft, good-natured; a big rough boy. Oh, and we also shipped three dogs. One belonged to Doderidge: Rowdy, the biggest and ugliest bulldog I ever saw, and all cut up with scars he'd got in fights. The other two were beautiful Newfoundland dogs travelling as passengers; they were for people in Greenock, and had addresses tied to them.

That's how it was the morning we left St John's with a big gale blowing from the nor'west, but that, of course, was a fair wind for us. Doderidge gave orders to loose the sails, but they wouldn't fall – all frozen to the yards. And we had to let them hang because if we'd pulled them it would have torn them to pieces. But once the sun was fully up they thawed a bit and we could finally work them, and by 4pm we had the foresail and lower topsail set, and the double-reefed mainsail. The wind now freshened even more, and as she was going dead square before it, this amount of sail was too much for the man at the wheel to make a good course as she was all the time griping her head round, and in the end we had to run the mainsail down.

Now it came on dark and now everything above the waterline was 'made white': iced. And by full night it was ten or twelve inches thick round the vessel, forward to aft. Only on deck where the water was washing aboard was it clear of ice, not having a chance to freeze. The shrouds themselves were ice-caked to about ten feet up the rigging. So with all this extra weight plus the weight of her overloaded cargo, she settled another foot and half, and now her decks were nearly level with the sea.

A big one came over the starboard quarter knocking in the window in the captain's room, and the window in the second mate's room (I escaped as the mate always has the port side). These 'windows' were little squares of glass with Venetian blinds, not the round ports you see on steamers these days. The *Elma* was what we call flush-decked: one deck from stem to stern with everything built onto it. So the cabin house, the six fresh water casks, all the spare spars and dunnage were torn adrift.

It was now coming on for eight o'clock and I was out on deck for the watch changeover. Doderidge comes out with his short, old, meerschaum pipe in his mouth.

'Looking pretty nobby, eh, Barnes?' he says.

'Some damn ugly-looking fellows rolling now,' I replied. The waves were rushing along the ship's side … washewww … like that. And they were going faster than the ship, which was doing about eight knots. You can always see a fast sea when it's running at night. It flashes like a flash of lightning when it breaks. And if it's a big sea it makes a noise in the rigging when it turns over.

We stood there for a time and eight bells rang, and I said, 'Now is the time to do anything that needs to be done while both watches are on deck.' I then added, 'Shall we heave her to?'

'Well,' he says, 'the other winter I had an awful gale coming up from the West Indies and she ran it out all right. We shipped one or two flobbers, but she took no damage.' Then he sees the main staysail sheet, which is what she would mainly be hove to under. 'Seedy looking,' he says.

'None too good,' I agreed.

'When the watch comes out,' he said, 'get that new coil from St John's, and reeve a tackle off and keep it as a preventer if we have to heave to.'

At which, I walked forward, and he went aft towards the wheel, and that's the last I ever saw of him. I was actually in the forward locker getting the rope, when I looked aft and saw this sea like a big white stone wall. I knew that once it came aboard everything would go.

And the captain, and the man at the wheel. I shouted the men to get up into the rigging, and jumped into the stays myself. Well, it came aboard with a sound like a wild bull and you could hear splinters breaking off the wheel, and everything making a noise, and the ship moaning like someone in pain. I couldn't see the cabin house, just the top of it over the water. And then she lurched over, and 'Christ,' I says to the fellows in the rigging, 'I hope she ain't going to turn bottom up.'

Now a ship is like a human being when she has more weight on her than she can bear; she will struggle to get up. And when I saw the rail come about a foot above the water, I jumped down onto the windlass, and hauled myself along using the heads of the belaying pins set in the rail, up to my chest in water. I knew I had to try to reach aft. Of course the wheel, wheelman, and Doderidge were gone, but the iron tiller was still there, going 'Swish!' 'Swish!' from side to side, but you couldn't go near it because if it struck you it would break your leg. But I was frightened if I didn't get it under control it might snap the pintals and carry away the rudder. So I took the main sheet, a two-inch rope, and watched for it to swing across to where I was, and took a quick turn around it. That put the ship hard-a-port and brought it onto the starboard tack. In the North Atlantic, in winter, that's the tack to be on. All right!

Now I roared to the men, 'Let fly them two foresheets!' Then they clewed up the topsail and then

I brought them aft to get the mainsail on her. 'Safe,' I thought.

I went to Doderidge's cabin to look at the damage. Under his bunk was Rowdy, the ugly bulldog. An old sailor, he was well jammed in; wouldn't come out even when we called him. The other two dogs had gone, of course – I knew that even though I never saw them going, and still don't know where they went. Doderidge's sextant was on the floor, all the quicksilver washed out – spoiled. So was mine. All the charts, eight or nine of them was washed from the rack and on the floor of his room – a mash and soaked with salt. One I carefully picked up was a general chart of the Atlantic Ocean and of St George's Channel between Liverpool and Ireland – now all I had to get me across. I got four fellows to hold it up against the galley bulkhead, as I thought the heat coming through the half-inch boards would dry it out. I then did the same with one of St George's Channel I rescued as well. As well as the charts, I had one compass left that was working.

I took full stock. All our kerosene oil was gone, smashed and run into the food stores. So there was now no way to light the binnacle, cabin, fo'c'sle, galley, or ship's side lights, leaving us in danger of being run down. But I thought of my father's ships, which were lit by small tin buckets with wicks, and filled with cod oil and seal oil, and of course we had casks of seal oil in our cargo. So that was all right.

All the water casks had gone over, but before we left St John's Doderidge had said, 'Begorrah! Them dogs will drink a lot of water,' and we had got the wharf cooper to make two portable casks and fit them in the aft locker. So that was all right. And a good job as we had no rain for the rest of that voyage. As for food, I've mentioned the kerosene, and at first it was retch and retch, but, d'ye know, after three or four days, we could keep it down, and after week the boys didn't care if it was good bread, or oil-soaked bread. Try it yourselves sometime and you'll see – it was like having relish on it. In fact, seventeen days later when we got to Greenock, and fresh food came aboard, it made us sick.

So now we rigged up a new wheel by squaring a barrel and nailing capstan bars across it, and using ratline ropes clove-hitched to the bars, and she began to move along again at eight miles an hour.

As to the ship's reckoning, I couldn't trust the second mate, so used to come out to heave the log myself every hour, though usually it is two hours between soundings. This meant little sleep, so I put Doderidge's nephew, Heck Campbell, on the wheel (who, it turned out, could steer pretty well), while I took to lying on Doderidge's bunk smoking and watching the compass, sometimes yelling up through the deckhead to Heck, 'Mind your steering there!'

Sometimes Rowdy, Doderidge's bulldog, would come in and sit down on his haunches, put up his nose, and 'woooooww' and whine as if to say, 'Captain Doderidge, where are you?' This generally made me feel awful bad, though once or twice I had a mind to heave him overboard.

This particular night I fell asleep, to be wakened by a yell you'd hear over five miles of ocean. I jumped up on deck, and there was the wheel going round by itself, and Heck Campbell with his two hands over his head, his mouth open and his eyes jumping out of his face. I shook him, saying 'What's the matter with you?'

'Uncle Hughie,' he said. 'Oh! Uncle Hughie!

'Captain Doderidge? What about him?' I asked

'I saw him! Standing looking at me!'

'Aw!' I said. 'It was because you were thinking of him.'

'No, sir. I was looking at the compass and slewed round and there he was, Uncle Hughie, looking at me.'

I began to laugh so it wouldn't encourage him, but his cry was so genuine I think he did see him. Anyway, I went back down to Doderidge's cabin, and lay on his bunk again. But to tell God's truth, for about half an hour, I lay watching the door thinking the poor fellow might be around that night and decide to pay me a visit.

After proceeding in this manner for two weeks or so, I reckoned we were getting over and might be north of Cape Clear. 'Tomorrow evening,' I said, 'we'll let the lead run down – try for bottom.' I knew by the colour of the water that where we were at, at that time, was 'off soundings'.

Next night we struck ninety fathoms. I didn't care now, I knew I was safe – and somewhere between Ireland, and Land's End, as I could see a whole string of nineties on the chart in a line across the Channel. But I didn't know how far north or south. So I decided to run the lead down again at 8pm, and then midnight: a lot of trouble, as the ship had to be stopped to get a true sounding. At midnight, I got sixty-five, and at four in the morning, fifty-six. I now put grease tallow in the hole in the bottom of the lead to see what was on the bottom. It came up sand and shells and I reckoned we'd soon see Tuskar Light. I lay down on Doderidge's bunk for a smoke, but fell asleep to be woken by 'Captain! Captain! Two lights about three points off the port bow.'

I went up for a look. 'Connybeg,' I said. 'Tuskar is white with a red flash every half-minute.' Then we raised Tuskar and I tell you I was as happy as a schoolboy. I shaped a course that put her up the Irish Sea between the Isle of Man and Ireland. By morning we'd passed the maidens off Belfast Lough. Then I shaped for Ailsa Crag and the Firth of Clyde and the Clock Lighthouse which I expected to reach about midnight, and at twelve sharp I rounded it. Now there was just twelve miles to go for the 'Tail of the Bank' and Greenock. Another three-quarters of an hour I was at the red light off the Tail of the Bank, and shortened sail, and rounded her to and let go my anchor.

At daylight a tug came out, and I sent ashore to James and William Stuart's office to ask where to dock – the west corner of the west harbour. So I hired a towboat to bring me up, and I made fast. The news soon got round there was a ship docked with her decks swept, and wheel lost, and captain washed away, and a jury wheel that looked like a bird catcher. It was in the newspapers and I suppose a thousand people came along to look at the ship. I later learned that every vessel that came into Greenock for a week before I arrived, and for a fortnight after, was wrecked in some way.

I got out all poor Doderidge's things, and dried them, and got them up the Stuarts' offices to be sent home. Then I telegraphed the ship's owners in St John's about the loss of Doderidge.

The reply was, 'Take charge. Do the best you can.' So now I was appointed captain. Next thing was repairs. The owners allowed me to put iron straps in her – I did so and got her all fixed up. Then I chartered a load of coal for Barbados. I sent to tell the shipmaster I would sign a crew the next day at 10am.

Next morning, I was up at the shipping office, and a crew was waiting. The shipping master shoved the articles to me, saying, 'Sign on, captain, please.' As I took the pen in my hand he said, 'Excuse me, captain, I'll need to see your certificate.'

'What?' says I. 'I have no certificate. The captain that

was lost coming over had no certificate. The laws of Canada and Newfoundland don't require one.'

'Well,' says he, 'you're going foreign?'

'Yes.'

'And under the British flag?'

'She's Canadian,' says I. 'The *Elma*.'

'No,' says he. 'You're a British ship going foreign. Here's the law,' he says. Then reads, 'Any ship over a hundred tons going foreign from the United Kingdom must have on board a certified captain and chief mate.'

'Well,' say I, 'I'd have to go to school for that, and can't delay the vessel.'

'Well,' says he, 'then I can't help. Can't sign this crew on.'

I went to tell my broker. He says, 'Barnes, this is a bad job. It would take you, I suppose, a month to get yourself up for school?'

'I don't know but I could pass now. I've been studying anyhow.'

He advised me to see the schoolmaster. I did, and after we'd talked he said, 'You could go up if you could give me three days with you.'

I said, 'The ship's ready for sea.'

He said, 'Do you think you could do it without going to school at all?'

I said, 'I believe I could.'

'Well, go and see the examiner,' I did.

'All right,' says the examiner. 'When do you want to go up?'

'Tomorrow if I can.'

'Right. Now I'll just see your papers.'

'What papers?'

'To show you've been six years at sea, and mate for the last two years. Your discharges.' I told him in those ships we didn't get discharges. It wasn't the practice. He asked if I could put myself out and get them. I told him not without writing to St John's, which would delay the ship for weeks. 'Well, captain,' says he, 'then I can't examine you. For all I know you *never were* at sea!'

'All right,' says I, and now told my broker I'd put another captain in her.

'Can you do that?' he asked.

'Of course I can,' I said. 'I'm captain of her.' I went out in the street and found an old Danish captain I knew, Johnson. We shook hands and I asked what he was doing.

'Nothing at present, worse luck.'

'Do you want a ship?'

'Where will I get one?'

'I'll put you in one.'

'How?'

'I'm captain of one at the moment, and can do what I like with her.' So I took him down and put him in. 'You'll have to take the same wages I was getting – as Doderidge was getting: £10 Canadian currency.'

'We get £10 out of England,' says he. 'That's £12 Canadian currency.'

'There's a lot of masters ashore here, Johnson,' I says. At this, Johnson makes up his mind he'll go.

So I left the *Elma* in Greenock as I couldn't even go mate in her, having no mate's certificate either. I went back to St John's as passenger in the *Meteor*. We struck ice and made a long passage of it. Off St John's a tugboat came out and heaved aboard a line. I was nearest and jumped out on a guy for it, and the tug sheered, and I was dumped on the deck of the tugboat. So I arrived back in St John's from a tugboat. The captain of the *Meteor* said later, laughing, 'My God, Barnes. You had a time of it this winter.'

5. Jailed in Aracaju from the *Mary* – we try to drown two soldiers – running out of food we live on sawdust.

AFTER THE *Elma*, I signed mate on the *Calderbank*. While she was loading I was walking along the street in St John's when I met Caleb Frond, whose brother-in-law was captain of my first ship, the *Mary*. Caleb was another Liverpool man, and the devil let loose. I hadn't seen him for years, but knew he'd never got any higher than bosun because he'd no education – never learned navigation. We went in a place and had a time, and I said, 'Come on, we need a bosun.'

We left September 1875, and met the autumn gales, and lost a lot of stanchions and bulwarks and finally made Pernambuco in forty days, and then charted for Aracaju, further up the coast, to load sugar for Queenstown for orders.

At the back of the sugar loading houses there was nothing but coconut trees with native huts here and there. These trees came down to within a hundred yards of the ship. Every night, when the breeze came, these trees would rattle a little, and to sit down and listen to them was music. The natives would gather and light fires, and all hands, the young girls, all, married and single, would dance and maybe play a banjo and their own instruments – queer things they'd play by rapping them together. The dance was what we might call a fandango and you'd crack your sides laughing to see them. They'd throw themselves into all shapes and forms, turning themselves nearly inside out.

We'd go ashore every night, and had our own girls, and I wouldn't interfere with another sailor's girl and he wouldn't interfere with mine. We used to call our girls our 'wives'. After a bit we got so we could dance the fandango better than the natives.

There was a fellow there, a Brazilian, who'd been steward for years in British ships. He got a bit of money, and a nice wife and some children, and opened a public house. Of course, this wasn't New York, this was Aracaju. We'd go there and get our drinks and he'd mark our slate until Saturday night when we'd get some money off the captain – but never too much.

Just before leaving, both Caleb and I wanted to get some cigars and stuff to take away, so we decide to beard the Old Man; his name was Cole and he was from Bideford, Devon, England: surly, but all right.

'What are you going to ask for?' said Caleb.

'Well, I don't suppose there's any use asking for more than ten shillings.'

'Well,' said Caleb, 'I want a box of cigars, cigarettes, and a lot of other things. Look. The more we ask for the more we'll get. Let's go for thirty shillings each.'

'Then let's get along now,' says I. 'Before the general crew gets there.'

Caleb went down. 'How much do you want?' says Cole.

'Thirty shillings.'

'Good Lord!' says the captain. 'What are you going to do with thirty shillings?'

'Oh,' says Caleb, 'three or four boxes of cigars. Cigarettes. Other things.'

'Here,' said the captain, 'here's a pound. Otherwise I won't have enough to give the rest of the crew.'

As Caleb came out he winked at me and I went in. 'Well, Barnes?' says Cole. 'I suppose you want money too?'

'D'you think I'm a hermit? What the hell is the use of earning it if you don't spend it?'

'How much?' asks Cole.

'Thirty-five shillings.'

'What!' cries Cole. 'I just gave Caleb a pound. I won't have anything left to give the men their last night ashore.'

'Twenty-five, then,' I said.

'I can't give you but a pound,' he says.

'You'd think it was your own money!'

'No need to get grumpy,' says he. Then, 'Here's twenty-five and keep sober.'

Now Caleb and I were away under full sail. We got

over town, and started in on this rum they called 'Casash'. Then heard some music and found this place where all hands were dancing. It was Saturday and everyone had just been paid. Them Brazilians are Portuguese descent, and all talk Portuguese though they're Brazilian. Half of them are white. And there they were, white and black, all dancing.

'Come on,' says Caleb. 'Let's have a look.' We went in and stood by the door, being strangers, but could see some of the girls giving us the eye. So now we each got a girl, and out onto the dance floor. Some of the men who'd been loading the ship was there – and, of course, friendly to us. But then one nasty fellow begins to make some sort of row and next thing we were fighting, and then this great big burly local that owned the house fired us all out. Caleb and the first fellow continued fighting in the street, and I got into it with another fellow and then along came the gendarmes – that's the police. They were in long light-blue coats that come low like an overcoat. They came up and began jabbering in Portuguese, and Caleb took a gun and bayonet from one and started to show him some English bayonet exercises. This other gendarme was about to run Caleb through when an officer appeared and took the gun from Caleb and told us in broken English we were arrested for causing a disturbance on the street.

'Come on, Caleb,' says I. 'It'll only mean one night in there.' So we went along, being prodded in the backside with a bayonet. When we got there I expected to go in the same cell as Caleb, but no, it was separate cells. Mine was nearly dark, no window, just a slit with bars across, and a bit of a candle that just allowed me to grope round the place. The door was a big plank with an opening about the size of your head with more bars. I was mad drunk and calling out all the names I could think of. The guard came down and put his fingers to his nose to me. After a time I got sick of that, and began to take stock of the cell.

I heard a sort of groan and walked over the window. I could see nothing out there. Then, by God! I saw something move in the corner of the cell – something like two bright eyes surrounded by hair and low to the ground. First I thought it was some sort of animal, then saw it was a human being crouched in the corner half-buried in old straw.

'Grrrrrrr,' he went. I could see he'd been there a long time, and wasn't friendly. I did all I could. Smiled, laughed, made signs, 'Grrrrrrrrr!' I thought I'd better leave him alone, and as I was pretty beat I leaned against the wall, afraid to lie down. I knew the place was crawling with vermin, and thought if I laid down I'd be picked up and carried away, and that the fellow in the corner might murder me in my sleep. So I chose a place and leaned flat against it, stiffening out my legs out like props. BANG! CRASH! I awoke to find myself on the floor and the savage from the corner standing over me. I sprang to my feet, he sprang back into his corner. I don't know which of us was the most frightened.

The noise brought in a soldier, and I told him the man had hauled me down. At this, the savage man began shouting that I had fell asleep standing up and then fell down – the soldier making signs telling me this. Then the soldier went, and the man and I got more friendly, both too frightened to be otherwise. At dawn I began to yell and sing, mainly to annoy them.

At ten, Captain Cole came. His salute was, 'How the hell did you get in here? Where's Caleb?' He thought we'd committed a murder or something.

'It was nothing,' I said. 'A row, and then got arrested.' I saw the ship's agent, and behind him the consul. Cole knew it was no good coming there without them. Them days, in Brazil, anyone English, Scotch, or Irish doing business, you might say they were like the governor of New York. They did what they liked because English money was behind everything. Next thing the door opens and we're out.

'You're all right now,' says the consul. 'But they're sending you back to the ship under armed guard, and don't want you back in this town.' All right.

We started back to the ship in this big Indian canoe, about thirty-five feet long, made from a corkwood tree, same as they've always used – one stroke this side, one the other, and you can't stand up, you'd go over. You had to crouch down. They sent two Pernambuco soldiers with guns with us, as well as the paddlers; one soldier in the bows, the other behind, us in the middle. Guns and bayonets and their great long overcoats, split tails hanging between their legs.

Caleb leaned across, 'We're about halfway. What d'you say we go over the starboard side and leave 'em to drown?' He was out of Liverpool, you know. But I was as bad – I just wanted it putting in my mind.

I said, 'Give the signal.'

He said, 'Make sure you fall with all your weight on the gunwale!' Then we stood and went over.

'Oh, Santa Maria! Santa Joseph! Dios! Dios!' That was the two soldiers screeching for all the saints in heaven to save them. Their guns had sunk, and they were hanging onto the bottom of the canoe.

'Let them drown,' said Caleb. 'Come on! Swim for the ship.' As we were climbing aboard, we could still hear them yelling, then saw a whole boatload of fellows coming off to pick them up. We were expecting them to come aboard and arrest us. But they mustn't have been anyone with sufficient authority as they turned back for the shore again.

We were pretty hungry by now, what with our night in jail, and went down to the pantry and had a damn good feed, then back on deck for a smoke. About five I looked shorewards to see a big lumber boat coming towards us black with soldiers. About sixty of them, the evening sun glinting off their bayonets. Says I, 'We're going to get butchered.'

'We can't fight them,' says Caleb, 'so best put on a bold face. What can they do? They picked up their men. We didn't commit murder. But I suppose they'll make a row.'

Then our men saw them coming, and got ready for a fight. But I told them, 'Don't interfere. Don't say anything.'

The officer and about ten more came up the ladder. He saw us on the poop but never made a move until he had about twenty or thirty on deck. Then he and two more came up onto the poop. He pointed at me, 'You bilota?' (pilot).

'Si,' I says.

'Arresta.' (arrested). Then to Caleb, 'You bilota?'

'Si.'

'Arresta.' As Caleb said, we couldn't fight that size of crowd. So we got into their boat and were marched through the streets, everyone stopping to look. This time they brought us to a more aristocratic jail. I had a room to myself with a bedstead and mattress. Caleb they took somewhere else. Of course, now I was sober I sat quietly, but thought to myself, 'It won't be so easy to get out of this one.'

And it wasn't. Apparently, when the captain came back aboard later that evening and heard what had happened, he was nearly crying. 'My God! What am I to do? Where will I get a mate and bosun? And the ship about to sail!'

So next morning he collected the agent, and the consignee, and came down the courthouse to try to influence this old courthouse judge. There was a hell of a lot of cross talk, but we were taken back to jail with the guards telling us we were to be sent to Fernando Noronha, an island convict settlement off Pernambuco, a very bad place.

About 4pm the captain reappeared, this time with the British consul. This latter was a sassy kind of fellow, a cockney, but he made use of the British government that day. He says, 'These men are British subjects off a British ship, who got to drinking liquor but have now done their time. And if you fall out with them, you fall out with the kingdom of Great Britain.' He says, 'You'll remember it all your lifelong years!'

That frightened the guts out of the old judge. However, he had to do something, so he made it as bad as he could: £10 each for the two guns that sank, to be paid on the spot. Captain Cole did so, and we set off back to the ship with flying colours. When we were back aboard we went to the rail and took our caps off and gave three cheers for 'Ingleterra!' And four days later were under way with all our girls up to their waists in the water holding out their arms to us; I felt like crying myself.

We had a pretty good run to Queenstown, and got orders for Bristol, and after the cargo was out I left the

Calderbank to go to school to pass for Master. To do so I boarded with a widow named Dowdel, whose husband had been captain of the barque, *Bernice*, out of Newport, Wales, and who had died at sea coming back from China. I stayed six weeks, and then my funds fell short, and I knew I'd have to make a trip to fill in.

I shipped in the brig, *Victor*, for Prince Edward Island. The cargo was pig iron, and we met nothing but storms, and at thirty days out the grub began to fail, and every five days or so we'd have to cut back some more. And not much water either. We had plenty of peas and rice to start, but after the seventy-fifth day everything ran out – nothing to eat now but headwinds and gales.

Then the steward was searching through the stern locker to see if he'd missed anything and noticed a bag. He put his hand in, 'Damn!' he says, 'That's bread!' He went to the captain and says he's found a bag he thinks has bread in it.

'Good God, Barnes!' says the captain 'That's bread we were going to give to the pigs when we had them. Let's see what it's like.'

There's 128 pounds in what we call 'a bag' of bread, and this was half full. We opened it. It was dark blue! With a sort of fuzz – whiskers – all around it. We took it up to the cabin and put it on the table to investigate further. Dark blue right through, except in the middle where it was bright green. I put a piece in my mouth. It was terrible.

The captain says, 'How about we get some soap and wash it?' Now the storm blew worse, and we knew we were going to have to eat it. So we'd fill a bucket with saltwater – the fresh water was almost out – and heave in the bread. Besides, we thought seawater might flavour it. Then we'd get a belaying pin and stir it till it went soft and mashy. We took this mash and strained it, then put some in the oven in a pan, and cooked it dry to a nice browny-green. When it cooled we'd grind it up in the mill, and with it we'd make what we called 'tea' in the evening and 'coffee' in the morning. Sometimes, as the cook had a whole barrel of pork grease (to sell ashore in the huckster shops rendered into little cakes), we'd put the mash in the pan with the grease and make what we'd call 'dandy-funk'. On this we now lived for another ten or fifteen days until even that ran out. Then the second mate said he'd heard people could live off sawdust. We had two big deck spars, one of which was spruce, and just looking at them you could see they'd last us about twelve months. So we had a man sawing all the time, with the sawdust dropping into a pan. We'd take this and put it in water for a time to swell it up and soften it, then that would go in the pan with more of the grease. The first time I tried it, I just shook my head – it was the hell of a thing. Just go to where someone's sawing spruce, and take a spoonful, and you'll get to know the taste. But after three or four days we didn't mind it no more than if we were eating pie. We were eight days eating it or die, and then ran ashore on Sands Point, Gulf of Canso, but we got her off after five days, and proceeded to Charlotte-town, Prince Edward Island.

There I left the *Victor* and signed on the *Model*, a brigantine, to run to St John's with a cargo of potatoes. Once there, I went up to school again, obtaining my captain's certificate on 31 December 1876. I then went sailing master in the schooner, *Cora*, of Greenock, in which I remained about a year and a half.

6. Girls – Liverpool girls – engagement rings – marriage.

WHEN I WAS first master of the *Cora*, at the age of twenty-six, I was courting the girl I afterwards married, Anastasia Frances Murphy. But before getting onto Anastasia, I want to say something about sailors and girls generally, and about Liverpool girls in particular.

As an apprentice, running out of Liverpool in the *Miranda*, if the ship was to be in port for some time I'd board with a Sam Weeks and his wife, a nice-looking woman with a big ringlet on either side of her jaw, Queen Isabella style. Initially, when sailors were 'homeward bound', just paid off with money, how nice Sam and his wife would be. Of course, once Jack was 'outward bound', his money out and the two weeks board he'd paid was up – well, nothing but black faces after that. Here's something I saw once. I was sitting inside the breakfast room door, smoking my pipe, and a fellow comes down. Late for breakfast, but very nice, some do that when in debt to the boarding-house master.

'Good morning, Mrs Weeks. Good morning, Mr Weeks.'

'So. What do you want for breakfast?' says Mrs Weeks. 'An egg? A herring?' (Of course, while you're homeward bound, it's ham and eggs all the time.)

'I'll take both,' said this sailor.

'Well, you're not going to get both.'

'All right,' said the sailor, 'whatever you want to give.'

I heard this, and thought, 'I'm flush, and not in debt to them. But if I was, they'd do the same to me.'

And now girls. Before I was married, before I had any particular girl, we'd pay off in Liverpool, London, Glasgow, New York, and 'run down the rag', as we'd call it: a theatre at night, then a bar to get drunk, and then a row. When the pay-off was gone, if you had a good suit, you'd pawn it, and when that was gone you signed on again. And when you left Liverpool, you might go round the Horn or the Cape of Good Hope … to China or Japan … maybe two years on a voyage. When we'd be away we wouldn't spend much money because we couldn't get much. Eventually, you'd head back for the home port, Liverpool, and pay off. This paying off was up at the shipping office where the captain would give you your discharge and you'd get back your discharge book. When you join a ship the captain keeps your book. If you run away and try to get another ship – the first they do is ask you for your book.

Now, at the shipping office, the shipping master says, 'Captain, what sort of a discharge do you want to give to this man?' The captain says either, 'Very good,' 'Good,' or 'Decline to report.'

The men now hurry off. Some have their wives waiting, married men. They are nabbed at once. Some have girls waiting. The rest club together and get up to a local gin mill, public house. There they have a fight to see who will stand the first drinks, then chat for a bit. Of course, the liquor isn't working yet, so everything is nice.

Then another fellow calls, 'The next drink is mine,' but as someone else wants to pay, the fun begins. As the barkeeper knows, there's still plenty of money there he doesn't call a policeman; instead he shuts the door.

'If you're going to fight,' he tells them, 'please wait until you're outside.'

Someone will say, 'Aw, forget it, let's have another drink.' Then they all get damn well crazy drunk and eventually he throws them out, and it's ten to one that two or three of them end up in jail. That doesn't mean all their money's gone. When they're searched the police find so much money left. All right. Well, they stay in jail till next morning, and then appear before the judge.

'What have you got to say for yourself?' he asks.

'Well, Judge, I paid off yesterday, and I've been out eighteen months … and you know how it is.' The policeman, if he's a good fellow, will give the judge a nudge. The judge is maybe another good fellow and understands.

'Five shillings or three days in jail.' That's all right. The bobby knows he is going to get a drink when they get outside. They all get fined five shillings, a dollar. Away they go. The cop is outside. He won't stand right in front of the door, but he's not far off.

They'll say, 'You're a damned good cop. Come and have a drink.' The cop will have a damn good belly-full before he leaves. So that's homeward-bounders.

Now girls. If the police see a girl holding up a sailor these days, they arrest them quick, but in them days a girl would walk up to a fellow and say, 'Hello, my beauty,' or 'That's my love.' And they would heave to at once, the sailors, and chat to them and get their eye on the girl they fancied, and link arms, and away they'd go.

In Liverpool, there was a lot of stores run by Jews them days. The sailors' boarding houses were Paradise Street, up Park Lane, Duke Street. The girls all used to live in a place called Copperas Hill; I don't know how it got that name – never found out.

Each girl wants to get her fellow clear of the others, because she's frightened the others might get something out of his pocket. They always find out his name first thing: Jack, or Tom, or Bill.

'Now look, Jack, I'm not going along the street with you dressed like that, you've got to get a good suit.' She knows she's going to get fitted out, too. 'Come on in here,' she says. Perhaps she knows this Jew and perhaps brings him men and gets something for it. In they go. Of course, by now, Jack has had two or three drinks.

'I want to serve you right,' says the Jew. 'I want to give you value for money. You like a navy-blue suit? A light suit?'

'Navy blue!' she'll say. 'Whoever heard of a sailor wearing light clothes?' She knows the navy blue costs more than the others. Jack never minds much about the price as long as it don't go over four or five pound.

The Jew says, 'There's this,' and 'There's that,' and 'That's about the best pants you can get in England.' Well, Jack don't care. Just runs it up and down his leg and that'll do. Now he wants a nice silk scarf.

The girl comes out with, 'I'd buy that myself if I had the money.'

'God damn it!' says Jack 'Get out two of them!' Everything she likes she's going to have one too. Now she has to get him out before he tries them on. He's proud of them, see, but if he sees himself in the glass he might buy something else, and she's afraid the money will go.

'We'll get the rest tomorrow,' she tells him. So he gets the clothes in a bundle, and goes out with it under his arm. He'll never think of buying sea-clothes until he's a day out, and feels the slap of seawater over him.

They go home to her house. She goes out and brings in a dozen of beer, perhaps two or three bottles of brandy. Mostly in England in them days it was brandy.

As a rule, nobody but a Scotchman would drink whisky. She wouldn't forget to have a couple of bottles of wine for her and her girl chum. They always had a girl chum they shared a room with, but the chum wouldn't be around the first day. So the girl and Jack would have the hell of a time during the day, and at night go to the theatre.

As a rule, £20 or £25 would last about three days, and Jack would see himself getting low. He'd begin to get mean, thinking, 'I've no boarding house yet.'

'Ah, damn it, we'll keep you when your money is out,' says the girl.

'What? No. No.' Bad as they were, they wouldn't bum off them girls. He'd say, 'I'm going down now to get a boarding house.'

'All right, I'll go with you.'

He'd go down and pay two weeks' board. He knew damn well tomorrow or the next day the money would be gone, and he wouldn't have a place to hang out. He wanted to get away in two weeks, anyhow, and he could last out two weeks in a boarding house. He's no money now, but that's all right because now I'm going to say something else. The girls them days were bricks, real bricks. I could go into the courthouse and prove it. Do you think that girl would leave him when he was hard up? Not a damn bit. If he was in his boarding house, if she didn't see him certain days, she'd come up and ask for Jim So-and-So, or Paddy So-and-So.

'Paddy, there's a girl out here for you,' the boarding master would say. Paddy'd come down and they'd go out.

'Come on! I have money if you haven't. Come on. I ain't going to see you on the beach!' And she'll stick to him till he gets another ship; never let him want for a drink, or for tobacco. She'll have others, of course. She'll tell him square. She'd say, 'Look, you know I have other men?'

Well, he wouldn't mind that. He'd say, 'I know that, Maggie,' or Mary. Or whatever her name might be. He'd say, 'That's all right.'

He knew what time to leave, see. As well as him, she might have three more on her hands during the day, all as hard up as he is, but she might also have two or three sailors' half-pay notes. Some of these girls would have half a dozen fellows' half-pay notes. The sailors that left their half-pay notes have gone away, they're out in India by this time, and when those notes come due she draws the money for a whole year, or two year, half their pay, see? And that's what she spent on these other poor swine. That was the stamp of girls that was going around. Poor, unfortunate creatures, but a good heart in them, you didn't have to look for it because everyone could see it.

Now back to Anastasia Frances Murphy. I had two rivals, Olsen and Kilgallen, both captains. Olsen was Norwegian, Kilgallen from Sligo. Anastasia's father,

Sylvester Murphy, was from Sligo as well, but didn't like Kilgallen. Olsen he plain despised because Olsen was Norwegian. But he liked me.

Anastasia's mother was another matter. She hated me as the devil hates holy water. And if Anastasia father's praised me, her mother would tell him he was worse than I was. She'd taken against me because Captain Laurie, who worked with Anastasia's father, and who was always up at the house, was always running me down, saying I was the leavings and scrapings of all the dirty ports in the world. And she believed him. So whenever Anastasia went into St John's for some shopping, the mother'd send the youngest son, Paddy, to follow her. And if Anastasia met me, Paddy would be right away home to tell his mother. Anastasia would get back, have her hat pulled off, and be given a good hammering.

Those times there was a big boat race in St John's harbour in the summer. Every ship entered a boat. St John's harbour is two miles nor'east to sou'west and you had to sail up the harbour, round a buoy, and back again. Well, we won the sailing race. Then we had to bring the boats into the harbour, strip the sails and mast, and then row them round the same course. And, by God, we won that as well! I was steering, and put my hand in the water to splash, to get some cool. An English captain saw this and accused me of using my hand as an oar.

He complained to the committee, who said, 'What the hell could he do with one hand?'

That night we were down at a bar called Foran's. The English captain came in and began blowing. I learnt he wasn't a captain at all. No certificate.

I was sitting with friends and heard him say, 'That Barnes was helping the boat with his hand.'

I jumped up and told him he was both jealous, and a dirty coward.

'What!?' says he.

Foran had a back room, and I said to this fellow, 'Come in here!' Then I told Foran to lock the door and let no one in. Well, I soon knocked the jealousy out of him – left him there all cut up, and with a black eye.

There was a ball next night to celebrate the end of the racing, and this captain and some of his friends (who were on the committee) said if Barnes is allowed to go to the ball, they would stay away. One of our St John's captains says, 'Look here, Barnes, stay away.'

'All right,' says I. 'I'm not here to break up the fun.'

Anastasia heard this and was in a hell of a way – she'd set her heart to go to this ball. Her mother asked another old St John's captain, Service, to take Anastasia. The ball was due to begin at eight. Going up the hill at six I met Anastasia and asked her if she was going, saying I wasn't.

'So I heard,' she said. 'But I am.'

'By God!' said I. 'If you had any spirit you wouldn't go!'

'I'm not losing fun for your sake,' she says.

'You can go to hell, then!' And I never spoke to her for eight or nine months, never looked at her.

Then Joe Murphy made it up with us. Joe was a friend of hers and one day kept me talking on the corner of Water Street until Anastasia and her girl chum came along. As they passed, Joe grabbed hold of her and said, 'What's the matter with you two? Come on, make it up.'

So I went home with her that night. Then I was going back to sea, and asked her if she would engage herself to me.

'Yes,' she said.

'All right,' says I. 'Tomorrow I'll buy a ring.' In those days a mate's pay was £10, and I got a whole month's advance and went to Jimmy Scott's jewellery store.

'Jimmy,' I said, 'got any good rings?'

'What sort?'

'Well, it might be an engagement ring.' He began to laugh, then showed me some rings. I tried one on the top of my little finger – at that time my fingers were all swelled up from knocking around at sea. I thought the ring about right, as it had two hands clasped in front of it. I thought it would just suit us. I paid about £5, then thought, 'Now I'll overstep the bounds and buy her something she doesn't expect,' this locket I'd seen where you could put a photograph in one side, and a snippet of hair in the other. Now I'd spent everything except six shillings. Just enough to get drunk. Pretty well every night in port I'd be drunk.

Now, to get to Anastasia's, because of her mother, we'd invented our own book of signals. There was an old watchman used to go up to tend her father's fire. Whenever I wanted to see her, I'd write on a wood chip 'Come down', or whatever, and he'd go up to tend the fire and slip her the one with the message.

She came down. It was between dusk and dark, and I won't say we didn't have a kiss or two, and then I gave her the paper with the ring in it, and a separate paper with the locket.

She pounced on the ring as a girl will, then said, 'What's this?'

'A ring,' says I.

'Aw,' she says, 'it's a regular cake. I wouldn't want that!'

'What?' says I.

'A regular cake. I wouldn't wear that thing.'

I grabbed it back, and the locket, and said, 'B'God! You won't wear either!' First I pitched the ring towards the water, but it didn't reach and fell on the edge of the wharf. Then I threw the locket which was heavier and went right into the harbour. She now ran for the wharf, having seen the ring fall short. But I was there before her and grabbed it.

'What did you do that for?' says she.

'I'm done with you,' was all I said.

She walked down the wharf and stopped at the end and turned and looked at me. I waited till she had gone, then walked down to the store at the end of the row.

It was kept by an old woman called Minnie Murphy, who sold fisherman's supplies and liquor on the side. She had a daughter named Annie, as pretty as any girl in St John's. Annie and Anastasia were what they call in New York 'girl friends'. So now I had two or three drinks and then called Annie over and gave her the ring. She put it on her finger and seemed quite delighted.

The next morning I came to the north side and boarded the *Cora* and didn't look again at Anastasia again for a couple of voyages. I heard later that the next morning after the argument Anastasia had gone to tell Annie about the ring. She saw it on Annie's finger and Annie told me, years later, Anastasia wanted it from Annie. But Annie said I'd given it to her, and she was going to keep it. Anastasia accused Annie of trying to steal me away, and they'd had a hell of a row.

Now Joe Murphy brought us together yet again, but somehow I had no courage to bring up marriage. Then, one summer evening, we were walking down by the Quidi Vidi Lake. It's about two or three miles long, and we went the whole way down one side, and almost up the other, and at last I says, 'Look here. We've been a long time beating about the bush. Will you marry me?'

She stops, and slews round, and looks at me. 'It's got to be one thing or the other,' I says. 'So what is it?'

'I'm satisfied,' she says. 'I was only waiting for you to ask.'

'Well,' says I, 'what about tomorrow night?'

'My God! That's quick.'

'But I'd rather no one knew till I come back next voyage. I don't want no one to know,' I told her. You see, the firm I was working for were very bigoted Protestants. I was mate in their *Petunia*, and expecting to be made master, and I thought my marrying a Roman Catholic girl might interfere with it. They might a get a down on me.

'If I do,' she said, 'marry you secretly, they'll kill me when they find out at home.'

'Be damned to them,' says I.

'We can't do it in St John's,' she says. 'Tell you what, we might go to Petty Harbour and have Father Welch marry us. I know him.'

'All right,' says I. 'I don't give a damn.' So we agreed for the next night and I contacted my captain on the *Petunia* and got for next day off.

Now I went to see Bishop Powers in St John's. I knocked at the door which was opened by another old priest, Father Forrester, an old busybody. Forrester says can he help me. I told him I was waiting to see Bishop Powers.

'What for?' he asks.

'Private business,' I says.

'Oh! But can't I do your business?'

'Nobody but Bishop Powers,' I tells him, and he walks off none too pleased. Now I'm invited upstairs to see Powers. I didn't know him, but my father and uncle did. And I knew he knew all our business, because our place was next to his. I told him what I wanted, and why I had to keep it secret.

He knew her family, of course, and her father. 'A fine decent man,' and asks why he, Bishop Powers, has never seen me before.

I tell him I'm a shipmaster and away a lot. He puts his arm round my shoulder, tells me my family, too, are fine decent people from Ireland, and that he'll give me a letter to Father Welch at Petty Harbour.

And now I goes to see a friend of mine with a carriage, Will Stevens, and says, 'Will, my girl and I want to go to Petty Harbour tonight to get married. Can you wait on the Esplanade, at seven, outside Carver's public house? I'll be in there having a drink, and she'll come along and climb in, and I'll come out of Carver's and climb in, and off we'll go with no one the wiser.' I then sent Anastasia a wood chip note telling her where to be and at what time.

At seven I was at Carver's, done up like a stick of chewing gum. Anastasia came down and off we went. About halfway there Stevens' old horse broke down and Anastasia began to cry.

'That's unlucky,' she said.

'Shut up, you fool,' I told her.

Stevens knew a farmer nearby, and we got another horse and tacked it on the carriage, and at Petty Harbour went to the priest's house, and Father Welch is there and I pulls out Bishop Powers' letter and give it to him.

'That's all right,' he says having read it, 'Now who have you got as bridesmaid?'

'No one,' says Anastasia. 'Won't your house girl do?' So he calls in this old servant, about forty, to stand by Anastasia, and Will Stevens stands by me, and we were married. I gave Father Welch £3 and he was delighted. Some didn't give half as much as that.

We started back for St John's and when we got there I said to her, 'Heave yourself out now. Go home to your mother.'

'Is that the way you treat a wife?' she asked me. Then went down the hill and home and hid her ring in the bottom of her box, and no one knew for three days. Of course, Annie, who had the first engagement ring, was told. Annie was courting Joe Downy, one of these straight-up-and-down fellows. He thought it a sin that I should go away, and Anastasia's people not know she was married, so he sent a bit of a note to the *Telegram* office (the newspaper) which read: 'Married by the Reverend Father Forrester in the Roman Catholic chapel of St John's, Newfoundland. William Morris

Barnes to Anastasia Frances Murphy, daughter of Mr Sylvester Murphy, South Side.'

A pack of lies. I left the ship that night to see her, and on my way called into Jimmie McKay's in Water Street. No sooner I was in the door then Ed Newman comes over and shakes my hand and congratulates me. I ask what's going on and he shows me the paper.

'If I get the fellow who put this in,' I says, 'I'll have him by the throat.' Now all the others ask me if it's not true. I tell them it's not, and it wasn't, being married by Father Welch in Petty Harbour. We all agree it's a nasty trick by someone, and I go out to meet Anastasia, as usual, at eight on Water Street, and see her running towards me, crying.

'Oh, God! It's in the paper! Mother will tear me to pieces!'

We turned off into Gower Street, and I says, 'You're not going home tonight. We're going to Mrs Hennessey's who has a room and bedroom furnished. You'll be safe there till I get back.' We went to Mrs Hennessey's and took the rooms, and I said that was where Anastasia would stay until I went away in four or five days' time, and where she'd wait until I came back.

There were some single chaps, engineers, staying there, and when I'd come from the ship I'd stop for a chat while they were having tea, before going upstairs to Anastasia. This particular evening the servant girl told me I was to go up immediately. I thought Anastasia was sick and bounded up and into the parlour, and there she was sitting with her mother.

I says to her mother, 'So you managed to get over?'

'I suppose I might as well now,' says her mother. But it's all right, and we have some tea. And her mother wasn't satisfied with Anastasia being by herself and made her go and live with them on the South Side until I got back.

I heard later that when her mother found we were married she sat in the chair screeching and crying until Anastasia's father came home. When he found what it was all about, he said, 'I'd rather take Barnes and put a shirt on him than that other damned Sligo hound.'

About that time I thought I'd also see Laurie, who was the one that first put me in bad with her mother. So I met him in Water Street and struck him between the eyes, and when he was on the floor said to him, 'You told lies about me, you swine. Now get up and tell some more.' But he never showed fight. Up and out as quick as he could.

Before Anastasia's mother died she came right round, and it was 'Barnes, Barnes' everywhere. She thought the sun shined out of me. And once the firm found out, it didn't seem to matter, for there was no trouble about my sailing on the *Petunia*.

That first engagement ring? Years later, Annie was dying of tuberculosis. I'd docked that day at twelve, and heard she wasn't expected her to live out the night, that the doctors had given her up, but that she'd heard I was back and would like to see me. I went up, and she took the ring off her finger and said, 'Poor 'Stacia. She always wanted it back, so here it is.' I took it, and then had a little talk to Annie, said my goodbyes and everything. I gave the ring to the other one, and she wore it sometimes.

And that's the whole thing about girls, engagement rings, and marriage.

7. Fever again – am pronounced dead before appearing for breakfast next morning – locked in the ice I have recourse to my wife's 'blessed candles'.

MY NEXT VOYAGE was as captain of the *Maida* and I left for Barbados with a cargo of codfish. When we arrived the authorities sent a note that the yellow fever was that bad that even the troops had been removed from barracks and tented out in the countryside. It also said that if I, or any of the crew came ashore, they would not give me a clean bill of health for any other island.

Well, we were not ordered on to any other island, and as I'd been long enough on board, yellow fever or not, I was going ashore. Out boat and soon I was there, and, as I know everybody around Barbados, I met Mr Clairmont, an old friend, who says, 'Ain't you afraid of the fever, Barnes?

'No, sir,' I replies. 'I've had a mess of it in the past and if I'm to get it I will, if not, I won't.'

I allowed no one else ashore, and we got the cargo out in eight days and took in ballast for St John's and left in a rain squall, myself at the wheel while the crew were getting on sail. I got wet through and went below for a glass of rum. I changed into some dry clothes and went back up, and about eight that night we were just off the end of the island, when I began to feel queer.

I said to the mate, Davis, 'I'm feeling damn bad, and believe I'm breeding the fever. I had it before and know the feeling.' He asked if we should turn back. 'No,' says I, 'we'll go on.'

I went down to my cabin and thought of a tale one captain had told me about having the cholera in Martinique, how he'd stood in his cabin like I was doing and having heard plenty of liquor was good for cholera, as much as you could, he put a bottle of brandy to his mouth and drank the whole of it. Then a full dose of laudanum, followed by one of castor oil. Then he'd jumped into his bunk and laid down. In the morning he got up, shook himself, and there was no cholera, all gone.

So I went to the medicine chest myself and got a dose of castor oil and drank it. Then I took a turn about the deck and came back down to the cabin where I drank a tumblerful of the rum then back up again. A quick walk round, then back down for a dose of laudanum. Then a big dose of salts. Then another glass of the rum and lay down. Then another tumblerful of rum. Then lay down once more with the bottle alongside me so I'd no need to get up next time.

Davis came down and asked how I was. I told him what I'd drank and he looked frightened to death. I told him if anything happened to me to get the vessel home. I then fell asleep.

At midnight Davis came down and, push or pull, couldn't wake me. Now he did get frightened. He called the second mate, and says, 'I believe the captain's dead!' The two of them called for the cook, and all three began pulling me nearly to pieces. All agreed that I was still warm, but that was because the cabin was hot. Otherwise I was dead.

The mate, Davis, says, 'We'll sew him up, and bury him at ten tomorrow morning.' Then went up on deck to tell the men. Now I'm dead, the crew began giving me a great name. 'A damned fine fellow', 'No nonsense about him', that sort of stuff. They told me later that Davis was assuming command before I was over the side.

Next morning the cook was laying the table for breakfast. At eight bells, 8am, he brought in the food and rang the cabin bell. This woke me. The cook was standing at the corner of the table facing the stairway. Next thing he saw me walking into the cabin. He dropped the bell and stood paralysed, his eyes out on his cheeks. At that minute the mate tumbled down, bosun right behind him. The mate saw me, let out a terrible yell, fell backwards and knocked the bosun flat.

Of course, I didn't know I was dead, and so just said, 'Are you all mad, or what?'

The mate says, 'We were looking to bury you in two hours, ten o'clock.'

'I hope you're going to give me breakfast first,' I said.

My next voyage on the *Maida* was Brazil and back in the winter. After thirty-six days homeward bound we caught the edge of the ice off Cape Chabereux, sou'west Newfoundland. There was about twenty miles of field ice and the *Maida* was copper-bottomed, and I knew if I put her in the ice I'd tear the copper off her, so I stood on and off for a day, the wind shifted, the ice parted, and I thought there was a channel to the land. I took the chance, but after ten miles the ice closed and jammed me up. I lay there for two days, and then a gale came on and jammed the ice even tighter, and as the sea got up the ice began to break up the ship. First the cutwater went, then the stem itself as far as the planks in the bow. We began to lay out wooden fenders which soon ground up, so now we cut up our big rope tow-hawser. We were at this all night, though I thought she'd be gone before morning. Now we hauled up some of our sails from the locker to make fenders of them as well. But luckily the wind dropped and so saved the ship from being crushed, but still we were jammed in. We drifted, ship and ice, to within ten miles of Cape St Mary. About six miles from this Cape are three rocks above water. The Bull, the Cow, and the Calf. The Bull is about ten feet above water; the Cow is about half a mile from the Bull. I could see from our drift we'd be between the Bull and Cow by night, and I did not know the depth of water between them. At 4pm, and about a quarter of a mile from them, I recalled there was a man forward who been in the seal fishery and was used to working ice. His name was Jack Angel and I sent him out on the floes with a lead line to sound when we got between the two rocks.

We got to them and he sung out, 'Five fathoms all along.' Thirty feet.

'All right,' I said, 'come back on board. We're going through.' You see, we only drew thirteen feet. But just in case I told the mate to put the boat over the side should we have to abandon her, and for the steward to get a big tablecloth and pack it with peas, and beans, and tinned meats, and then to tie it up and heave it into the middle of the boat, and a canister of tea and coffee (if we can't boil it up, we can suck it raw) and a keg of water. Then I went below, put my hands to my head and tried to think of anything else. I had this big, new, English ensign. I laid it on the cabin table, then went to the locker and got a ball of twine and laid it beside it; then some Minard's liniment and Radway's Ready Relief from the medicine chest, then a hammer and a box of two and a half inch nails.

I ran up and asked the mate where we were. He told me we were about halfway along the Cow – still clear. I ran back below and now it struck my mind – the chronometer. This stood on a chiffonier, a chest of drawers you'd call it. The chronometer was in a box padded with green baize. Also in there were two pieces of blessed candle – my wife would always put them there when I went to sea; the Catholic Church, you know.

Seeing them, I thought of my wife and the words she'd always say, 'If you get into trouble light them!' So I lighted one and turned it upside down to let the wax puddle onto the chest of drawers, then stuck it there. Then I folded everything in the ensign and tied it round my middle so I looked like two men.

Just then, the cook, Tommy, ran down. 'Captain! Captain! The mate says we're running clear!'

I jumped up and stood on the fo'c'sle as she came to the end of the Cow, gave a quick jerk with the tide, then swung clear. Now there was only picking up Cape St Mary and avoiding Point Lance to worry about. That came just before daylight. I glimpsed a white spot of cliff.

'Good God,' I says as we drifted by at about fifty feet, too near to land for any ship. And then we were in St Mary's Bay, but with a drift of about forty miles before we got to its end.

So I called to the mate, 'Davis! We're clear! The next place we'll hit will be Red Island at the end of the bay. Come on down to my room.' Once there I took out a bottle of rum. I didn't think about touching it while we were in danger, but now I said, 'We're going to have a good drink and then you can turn in.' And we did, and he did.

The next day broke beautifully and we were almost up to the Bay Head when an opposite gale came on and by 4pm we were almost back at the Bull and Cow. The second mate went crazy, and ran up the rigging shouting, 'We're going onto those rocks again!'

I said to him, 'Time to bid the Devil good morning when you meet him.' Then I said, 'You damn fool! D'you think bawling halfway up the rigging will stop us going on them?'

However, we cleared right through, then found Placentia Bay, and in about four or five days were up to the head of that, about eighty miles. Then another nor'easter and I was back down again. At that I made up my mind to run for Burrin or St Lawrence.

I said to Davis, 'If we can get her out of this ice, we can beat up to St Lawrence and get that stem fixed.' So I had the men lay a chain mat across the stem, and shift the ballast a bit more, and I beat her up to St Lawrence, a fine straight harbour six miles long.

In St Lawrence I knew a man, a Italian merchant, Gregory Giovanini, an old friend who I'd often had a drink with in St John's. The wind had now dropped and I said to Davis, 'If it's this calm in the morning I might be able to get help to tow her up to Point of Beach, where we can fix the stem. I know a gentlemen here who might help, so get the boat, I'm going ashore.'

We rowed up, and there were several little wharves, but I chose the best kept, as I knew Giovanini and his brother were the best-off people there. I asked some men who were smoking on the wharf, and one had heard my name and took me up to the house. Giovanini opened the door – he must have been eating as his mouth was chock full.

When he could speak, he said, 'Good God, Barnes. Where have you come from?' Then, 'Come in.'

He introduced me to his wife, Maggie, I'd not met her before, and I said, 'I'm all broke up,' and told him my story.

His wife said, 'Ain't you going to have something to eat?'

He says, 'How many men have you ashore?'

'Two,' says I. He says he'll go and find somewhere for them, and that I'll be staying with him that night. So he went off, and when he got back his wife's sister, Lizzie Fitzpatrick, just out from the convent in St Pierre, played the piano and we had a hell of a time, and I was still asleep next morning when he caught me by the leg.

'Come on,' he says. 'Come on!'

We headed down to the wharf. It had frozen the previous night and there was a scum of ice about half an inch thick over the harbour. I though we'd never do anything now as it was about five miles to the *Maida*. But on the wharf, waiting, were a hundred men who, Giovanini told me, were going to get my ship up.

I looked at him, 'What's it going to cost, Grig?' I'd known him a long time.

'Nothing,' he says. 'Just leave them alone.'

They broke a channel through the ice by hitching their boats together. It's not very thick, saltwater ice in a bay or harbour. Once on the *Maida* they ran forward to the windlass and began to heave, every man of them. While this was happening Grig and I went down to my cabin and I broke out the Brazilian casash. I knew I didn't have enough on hand to treat the crowd, but I also had two sixty-gallon casks buried in the ballast in the main hold. I told the mate to take some demijohns, and fill them from those casks.

In the meantime Grig's men got their boats line ahead and were rowing hard; the ship was moving forward as if being towed by a tugboat, and by three o'clock we were anchored at Beach Point.

It was St Patrick's Day, and I said to Grig, 'Them men have acted decent by me, and, by God! I'll act white by them.' I told the cook, 'Get out some mugs and a couple of cans of fancy crackers, and one of those red Hamburg cheeses. And then call all them men along.'

They came, and we had a damn good drink: all merry drunk, not falling-down drunk, merry drunk.

'Now', Grig says, 'we'll go ashore to see Pike,' who owned the repair stage, the only place we could fix her stem. Pike was near seven feet tall with big whiskers that came down to his middle and up to his eyes and which were wavy, and, just like the sea, speckled with grey here and there: 'Protestant whiskers', they used to call them. He was about fifty and married to his second wife, a young girl of about twenty-six. His mother, and an old woman, were there also.

We had to bargain with him. 'Captain,' he says to me, 'there is a bore – a sort of tidal wave – comes here every now an' then. And when it come it tears everything to pieces. And if it comes in while your ship is tied to my wharf which is connected to my house, why, both my wharf and house will end in the harbour. So look, I'll run the risk, but you'll have to pay me £5 a day while she's at the wharf, and if the bore comes the ship's owners must replace all my property. Will you sign a bill on it?'

'Any damn thing you like,' says I.

Well, we fixed it, and after six weeks the wind came off from the nor'west and the ice began to move off the land. We hove up and we had all St Lawrence to help us out, and Grig was the last to shake hands with me.

When I got back the owners were well pleased for getting the job done, as it meant there'd be no delay in loading her again right away for the West Indies, which they immediately did.

Of course, I had to tell my wife all about it, and about the candle; how it had burned down and ruined a good chest of drawers, leaving a big black mark.

'That's what saved you,' she said. 'That and nothing else. But you don't believe it, do you, you heathen?'

'No,' I told her, 'I don't.' But I did think about it.

8. I turn shopkeeper – W M Barnes, groceries and provisions.

PEOPLE OFTEN ASK do sailors ever wish to get away from the sea – start a business onshore – something like that. Often when I'd get a big puncheon of water over me after turning out of a warm bunk, I'd say, 'By God! I'd like to get clear of this.' But once ashore, after three or four weeks, all I'd want was another ship, restless to be off again.

But I remember when I once fell out with my owner, and there wasn't much doing in St John's, plenty of captains and mates on the beach.

It had been a month, and my wife said, 'You've no ship and your money's out. Go see your father about starting a business. He's just sold some property on Barnes Road for £2,500. He made a fortune. Why can't you?'

I thought it over then went to see him, my gills out ready for a fight.

'Good day, Father.' He looked at me.

'Hello, Will.'

First I stood like a stuck pig, then at last yelled, 'Father, I came to get some money from you. To open a business.'

'Where would I get money to give you?'

'That property – £2,500.'

'I did. But don't intend to squander it.'

'Look,' I said, 'I'm pretty hard up. And there's no call for masters, nor mates. So I'm asking you to lend me some money to open a grocery business.'

'Not a public house?'

'A grocery store!'

'Who's going to run it?'

'I am.' He put his hands on his hips and laughed until I thought he was going to cry. I said, 'Hell's flames! If you weren't my father I'd knock your block off!' Then added, 'If poor Mother was alive, she would kill you with the first thing she could lay her hands on.' He sobered up right away.

'You're sure you're not intending to sell liquor or rum?'

'Not even to make money. I couldn't sleep if I did.'

'All right,' he says. 'Come back tomorrow.'

The next day, my aunt gave me £200 from him. He wouldn't come himself because he knew I'd grumble it was too small. It was not enough to fully open a grocery store, but I could make some sort of appearance.

I went to see young Walter Grieve, general wholesaler and nephew of old Walter Grieve, the man who'd broken my father's business. I told him what I was going to do, and he laughed harder than my father. When I got angry he said, 'Barnes, I wasn't insulting you. Just picturing you behind a counter instead of a ship's wheel. Now, you've got £200. If you take £200 worth of goods from me, I'll allow you another two hundred credit. And when you pay a hundred of that back – you get fresh credit. How's that?'

I said, 'All right, sir. Thanks.'

The first thing was to get a house over a shop. My wife thought we would do best on Water Street. We found a place and I got a sign painted: W M BARNES, Groceries and Provisions. We got shutters in place, about eight of them. And I got shelves up and started placing things round them. In four or five days everything seemed right. The people were all dying to see inside, and finally the day came.

'We'll open first thing tomorrow at 6am,' says my wife.

We went to bed, and next thing was a hammering in my ribs. 'Hello?' says I.

'Ain't you going to get up?' says my wife.

'Ain't you going to lend me a hand?' I replies.

'Ain't you big enough to manage the shutters yourself?' I began to shave while my wife, like all women, was up and down with excitement. She said, 'You think you were going to a ball instead of taking down shutters.'

'God damn it!' I replied. 'I would rather face a regiment than have the public watch me do this. Can't you do it with the girl?'

Said she, 'You were quick enough to get a shop and now you're saying you don't want to open it?' Then she dumped herself in a chair and screeched out laughing.

I could stand it no longer, but ran downstairs, and, as I could see no one coming, began on the shutters. They must have got a fright being torn down and pitched through the door like that.

Four or five men came along going to work. Some said, 'Good morning, Captain Barnes.'

I thought they were making fun of me, and shouted, 'Go to hell!' I began to yell for my wife. She came down, and I told her for Moses' sake to take the shutters out back, while I got the rest down. She called for the hired girl and I could hear both of them laughing. I'd just got the last down when Captain Russell comes along.

'Good Lord, Barnes! What are you doing?'

'You go to hell, too,' I said, and flung the last shutter so hard it almost broke my wife's shins.

Then I stamped inside and up and down and she said, 'Don't go through the floor.' This shop, see, had a very weak plank floor.

I was just about to warn my wife not to go any further when a woman comes in. My wife at once goes to wait on her, and I go in the back. Then my wife comes in back and says, 'Are you going to let me do it all?' I went out and stood in the doorway.

Then a woman comes in and says, 'Good morning,

Captain. A pound of butter, please, and two pounds of sugar.'

I went to the butter pail, gouged out a big chunk and threw it on the tin scale. My wife, looking over the glass door leading out to the back, said, 'Aren't you going to put any paper under it?' This paper came in sheets of dirty yellow colour, and you'd tear the sheets off a large pad as you would letter-writing paper.

I said to the woman, 'My hands are clean, missus,' then put the paper under the butter and flattened it down. It took me along time to make the weight. Then I went to the sugar scoop. I made the two pounds and folded a paper to pour it into. Turned over the ends and laid it on the counter and began to tie it with the twine – but this broke and now the sugar began to come out. I shoved it in with my hand and now tried cross-lashings on it, but could never handle knots in string and hauled it too taut and it fell off the counter and there were two pounds of sugar on the floor.

The wife rushed out shouting, 'For heaven's sake!' while I let out a terrible oath and rushed out the back and made a start at the girl, who ran into the shop.

The wife and girl were now both in the shop afraid to come out back. Eventually they scraped up the sugar and came through for breakfast, but were now too frightened to laugh. They'd had a good look at my face.

Every day it was one row after another. She'd never leave more than six or seven dollars in the till, but I needed my grog three times a day: mid-morning, midday, afternoon. 'It's either the grog or back to sea,' I'd tell her.

Business began to pick up: plenty of custom, but that custom wanted to run up bills. We would trust them, but when they owed about ten or fifteen dollars they'd disappear.

Saturday there was these public sales and auctions, and the wife would usually go to them after studying in the papers what was to be had. This Saturday it was raining like the devil, and she had a cold coming on, and asked if I would go. I wouldn't have her out in the wet, and agreed. She wanted a barrel of onions, a box of soap, a barrel of oranges. She gave me ten dollars. I went down to Green's, the auction place. Who comes along but an English captain named Axford who couldn't get a ship either, and now kept a crockery store. Like myself, he'd been sent by his wife.

We stood side by side and I said, 'I don't like the look of them oranges.'

He said, 'And it's so cold. Let's go have a drink, Barnes.' We went to Tom Capen's. We stood one each, then Kennedy comes along.

'Hello, gentlemen,' he says, 'have one with me.' Kennedy worked at the water company where he eventually spent most of their money and was asked to leave.

Then Axford and I went back to the sale for the onions, but they were small ugly things and Axford said there was another sale at Deering's, where he'd heard there was some bargain tripe, of which he was very fond. We went down and the tripe was in big stone jars, cemented down. It came out from England as they don't put up tripe in our country.

Axford says, 'No one here eats tripe. It will sell cheap. Will you take half a jar with me?'

I told him I couldn't take it home, but if he took the jar to his house, I'd come across that night with a bucket for half of it. After that we went back to Capen's to 'wet the tripe'. Sage came in and I told him he was just in time to order some 'noggin' – that's rum with hot water we drink in winter. As it was raining heavily outside we stopped for another few drinks. Then Axford says, 'There's another sale uptown at Curran's on Water Hill.' There was nothing much there except a great big horse that looked badly attended to, pretty raw on his bones, worked almost to death.

Curran says, 'Folks! I have a horse here! A horse I'm going to put up!'

No one said anything for a time, then one fellow says, 'Four dollars.'

Curran rapped his pencil, and looked round, and suddenly I say, 'Four-fifty.'

The other fellow added a further fifty cents. 'Five dollars!'

Now I'm bidding, I won't be beat, and goes, 'Five-fifty.' The horse was knocked down to me and Curran

asked if I'd take it with me. I said I was in the process
of sorting a stable, but would be back that evening.

Sage now says, 'We might as well wet the horse.' We
went to Sandy Rankin's and Jim Morgan, the cooper,
came in. When I was drunk as I could be, I decided to
set off home. On my way I met Captains Byford and
Searle, two old friends. I told them I was going home,
but they wanted me to have a drink. At five o'clock in
the evening I had about twenty-five cents from the ten
dollars my wife had given me. I went back for the horse
and Curran asked what I had to put on him. I told him
nothing, and Curran loaned me a set of blinkers, a
bridle, and a bit, but I must handle them carefully and
bring them back to him. Curran's man rigged the horse,
and they brought me a box to stand on. I mounted up
and there was no saddle and his backbone as sharp as
a razor. We set off with all hands yelling, 'Hard-a-
starboard, Barnes!'

To get home we had to go up a big set of wooden
steps which weren't built with horses in mind, but he
knew what was expected of him and got up them fine.
We jogged along with people shouting I'd stolen him,
and soon we turned into Water Street. Our place was
second from the corner, the corner shop being a
butcher named Keefe. He knew about our weak floor,
and when he saw me position the horse on a course for
our door, yelled, 'For God's sake! You'll go through
down into the cellar!'

'Aw, go to hell!' I said. 'That's where I want him!' I ran the horse into the shop, and the top of the door took me off over his backside. He ended up inside, and me sitting on the step.

My wife and the girl were, as usual, in the back, looking over the glass, and Anastasia shouts, 'What are you doing with that horse?'

'Putting a tackle in the loft, to lower him into the cellar, to eat this winter,' I told her. She told me later that after I'd said that, she knew I had the 'horrors' with the drink.

I now tried to pull him out. But he sensed the floor was unsafe and was snorting and geeing with fright. Keefe, the butcher, came in and says, 'Turn him, captain, and lead him out.' First the old horse put one hoof in the stove, then the other, but we finally got him about. At which point Keefe suggested I bring him to Keefe's slaughterhouse where he'd find him a place.

I lodged him there, but only for the night, then went home to face my wife. Next morning I took it to a place where horses were boarded. The daily rate was twenty cents plus ten cents for oats, and ten for hay. When I'd go to the till for the money for the horse, Anastasia and me would fight. This went on for a week. It got so much I knew I'd have to sell the horse. Anastasia said I'd be lucky to get two dollars.

I didn't know what to do with it, to tell the truth. Then, going down the street one day, I met Stephen

Trench, a North Island man. Trench would come up, spring and fall, to buy his stocks. We got to talking and he said he'd like a cheap horse to drive home the sixty miles or so to where he lived. 'Then,' he said, 'I'll shoot him and salt him in barrels to feed the dogs in the winter.' They have lots of dogs there to haul wood in the winter as there's no coal to be had.

I told Trench about the horse and that he could have him for what I paid: five dollars fifty. He came to see him and took him on the spot. I paid off my last debt to the stableman.

I went back to the shop and threw the five-fifty down on the counter. 'Let this be the last I hear of that horse,' I said to my wife.

Next spring I met Trench again on the street. 'Damn you,' was the first thing he says. 'That old horse died on me halfway home, and I had to buy another to get my stocks back.' But the horse was bought square, and sold square, and Trench knew it, and I took him for a drink, and that was that.

But the shop wasn't doing so well, and wasn't going to pay enough to keep me on shore, so I asked around. An old friend, Captain Davidson of the *Feadore*, said he needed a mate. I went home and said to my wife. 'Enough's enough. Get my things ready. I'm off tomorrow in the *Feadore*.'

9. Like a snake walks – *Corinne*.

AFTER A COUPLE of trips in the *Feadore*, I left her to sail mate in the *Gratia*, Captain Manning. We ran into a hurricane and the ship was badly knocked about and we had to put into St Thomas, Virgin Islands, West Indies – in those days under the Danish flag. St Thomas was a great port for wrecked ships to come into, while waiting for those ships were all the land sharks in existence. Seeing the wreck coming in they only wanted a quick look at her captain to see whether he was a young green master who might be used to rope his owner in for hundreds of pounds, or an experienced man who had been through the mill and could fight them off.

But sometimes it's the owners themselves who are crooked and the captain, experienced or not, loses his wages. Here's what happened to me on a voyage that was crooked all the way through. The consignee was crooked, the owner was crooked, and, besides that, the ship's bottom was full of wormholes as crooked as the letter 'S'. These worms, you see, enter a plank under the water but they don't bore straight as you would with a gimlet – they bore like a snake walks and from where they enter to where they come out on the inside might be five feet. It might also enter as a small worm but by the time it eats its way though those five feet it will be a big worm and cause a big leak.

Once in St Thomas we found several Nova Scotia vessels there, all as leaky and dismasted as we were. Also in the harbour was a brig called the *Corinne*, owned by a Frenchman called Marvelle. They loaded her and she leaked. They put her in dry dock and worked on her and brought her out and she leaked some more. And at that the captain left her; he either just got tired of it, or just cold feet.

Marvelle now began speaking to a friend of mine, Captain McDonald of the *Humber*, saying he didn't know what he was going to do as it would cost a lot of money to bring a skipper down from New York. McDonald mentioned me, and that I'd an English captain's certificate. Marvelle asked McDonald to talk to me, and he came on board and says there's a captain's job waiting for me on the *Corinne* – cargo for Boston.

I spoke to Captain Manning who said, 'She's had a couple of captains now – none of who would have left without good reason. And damned if I know how she'll get to Boston with those leaks.'

'Well,' says I, 'maybe one man can do what another can't. Surely you won't stand in my way?'

'What will you do for a mate?' he asks.

'Tom Tarrant, our second mate,' I says. 'As able to sail mate as I am, maybe better.'

'Then I'll be short a second mate,' says Manning, 'but all right. Go on,' then added, 'but you'll never see Boston in that thing.'

'You won't be blamed for it,' I told him, and went ashore to speak to Marvelle. We went privately to his office where he told me all he'd had done to try to repair the ship. He seemed a very fair kind of man.

'Go aboard and look round,' he says, 'There's a man there called Louie. A French sailor who's watching things for me. I recommend him as a good mate. Talk to him then come back and tell me what you think.'

I went on board and Louie took me round and I drove my knife into all the covering boards and waterways and deck seams – if a ship is slack your knife will go in, and the pitch in the seams will be cracked. Then Louie got out the jollyboat and we rowed round the ship and I jammed in my knife in here and there, and that seemed solid as well. I went into the hold and sounded her with a wooden maul – you can tell by the sound whether there's a weak spot in the timbers. The only thing I couldn't see was the bottom of the hold because a lot of cargo was in covering it. I came to the conclusion the leak hole was made by a worm and we couldn't see it because the *Corinne*, under the water, was painted black and covered with grass. I asked Louie when he'd last pumped ship.

'This morning eight o'clock,' he said.

'Did you count the strokes?'

'No.'

'All right,' I said. 'It's midday, and you and I will pump her now.' We pumped her out until 'we got a suck' – that is, until she was dry, and then I took the pumps and locked them in the captain's room so no one else could pump her. I came back at 4pm and we pumped again and it took about three hundred strokes to get a suck, but that's nothing at sea. I reckoned one man pumping every two hours could keep her dry.

I went back to the *Gratia* and told Manning I was going captain in the *Corinne*. His lip dropped. I then saw Marvelle and we agreed seventy-five dollars per month as my wages, and half the passage money (she carried four passengers and if I could get any I would get half of what they paid). He also said he intended keeping her running between Boston and St Thomas, and that, as St Thomas was a free port, I could bring out anything I liked to sell, and he wouldn't want any freight on it.

In three days they finished loading her with old iron, coconuts, old bales, and other wreck material. Marvelle then called me up to his office to sign the bills of lading. An old clerk brought them out and the bills read that everything was 'in good order and condition'. The old clerk tapped Marvelle on the shoulder and they walked away for a conversation I couldn't hear, but I did catch something from the clerk about 'not serving the captain that way'. I saw Marvelle shrug his shoulders. I thought about all that cargo I hadn't been able to get a look under, and so asked Marvelle before I signed if everything *was* in 'good order and condition'. He assured me it was, that the cargo in question was shelled coconuts which came out of a wreck, so they had been under water, but that their eyes weren't broken, and even if some did let in water they would be dry by the time we got to Boston. Eventually I signed, after he'd agreed to my putting in a clause saying the coconuts had been under saltwater.

The next thing was to get a crew. This took me a week, back and forward, ship to shore, day and night. One evening I came off a little earlier than usual. There was no sign of Louie at the gangway and I made no noise coming on board, though this was not deliberate. I saw him at the starboard rail and heard someone talking. Then saw Louie picking up coconuts and heaving them down. I jumped across the deck as Louie slewed round. I looked over the side and saw one of the day labourers – a yellow nigger with long black curly hair, I forget his name.

'This is nice work,' I said to Louie. 'Robbing the cargo. Well, you'll go to jail for it in the morning!' I looked down into the boat, 'And you, too!'

Louie began crying, and the other one began crying. 'Oh, Captain! For God's sake! Oh, mamma! Mamma!'

I went down to the cabin, and when I came up an hour later they'd both gone. Next morning I told

Marvelle about the man he'd recommended to me. He said he was going right up to put the law on them. He did and they were taken up, and I had to go and give evidence. The yellow feller was the only support of his mother, and between the jibs and reels he was let off. Louie drew three days in jail.

I got a mate called Simmonds from Saba Island, and with him four crew members. But after they'd pumped her twice in one day the four crew disappeared, though Simmonds stayed. I went ashore and collected four more, and was on my way to the shipping office, when a gang of about a dozen niggers, standing on a corner, said, 'Hell, boys! That thing's full of water. Gwine to sink, she is.'

Unable to stand it any longer, I cried, 'You black swine. If I had a gun I'd fix you.' A Danish policeman across the street came over and they all scattered, my new crewmen with them.

After a lot of hard work I finally got a second crew mustered, but after sampling the pumping they cleared out, too. The last crowd I got the night before sailing – at the last minute – when there was no pumping to be done, and told the mate, Simmonds, and second mate, not to mention pumping. Next morning I got the anchor up, and the wind was right, so I told Simmonds I was going across to another ship where my chronometer was being checked, and not to let anyone ashore under any circumstances.

When I got back, I laid the chronometer on top of the cabin house, and said, 'Mr Simmonds. Let go the line, sheet home your square sails!'

He says, 'De cook's ashore, sir.'

'What!' says I. 'Didn't I tell you to let no one ashore?'

'Look, captain' he says. 'When you left he had de coffee all ready, an' brought it down de cabin, sir, and me an' de secon' mate went down for our coffee and thought de cook was in de galley gettin' breakfas', and didn't know but while we were getting's our coffee a boat came passin' which de cook hail de boat an' jump in an' I didn't know but wat he's goin' ashore to buy somepin ...'

I swore like a madman, but said to myself, 'By God if I go ashore to look for the cook, the rest will be gone by the time I get back.' I thought quick. I was tied to another ship and usually would have to go across in the jollyboat to loose the lines, at which point any in that boat could pull for shore. So I whipped the line off the chock and let it go over the stern.

'Now!' I cried. 'Sheet home them square sails!' She began to move, and now it was mutiny if they disobeyed an order. And before they could move, I was right among them. 'Look, men,' I said, 'I can't go ashore looking for another cook. She'll go the way she is and I'll do the cooking myself if needs be, and pay the cook's wages between ye all when we get to Boston.'

I told a man to take the wheel, and took the

chronometer down to the cabin, then ran back up in case he decided to put her on the rocks. The breeze began to freshen, and outside the heads she began to dance along at eight or nine knots. And there wasn't that much wind. So I went to the stern and looked at what should have been white water, but was more like a green field. All the grass was now washing off. This, of course, opened up the leak up some more. By evening we could hardly get a suck on her. She was doing eleven knots and it was impossible to pump her dry.

Next morning, about four, I was lying on my sofa in my room, and I reckoned we were about sixty miles off Abaco. Now she'd been carrying wood and was consequently was full of all sorts – scorpions and centipedes and great big spiders and rats. So much so I was frightened to lie in my berth, preferring the couch where I could watch them all going about their business up and down the white zinc-painted walls.

The mate, Simmonds, came in and told me the men were pumped out after working it all night, and had knocked themselves off.

'What?' I cried. 'There's nothing but pump or sink, Mr Simmonds. Nothing!'

'How far the nearest land, sir?' I could see he was thinking of Abaco sixty miles away.

'Hundred and twenty-five miles,' I says. 'Abaco.'

'Hundred and twenty-five miles?'

'Maybe even more. Pump or sink, Mr Simmonds!

Pump or sink!' He turned away, and I knew I had to act fast. There was a big American axe, the red paint wasn't worn off half the blade, and there was a crook in the end to stop it slipping out of your hand if you made a heavy blow. I took it up, and followed Simmonds out. I knew I had to quell the mutiny that was brewing or die in the attempt. As Simmonds reached the forward end of the house to speak to the crew, they saw me come up with the axe over my head. They all stood back.

There was one big nigger there who had been in British ships and was a sort of sea-lawyer: that means a fellow always getting others into trouble from listening to him. He'd told me himself he'd been in the Liverpool barques. He was the only one who frightened me. But I knew I had to frighten the others first so I swung that axe round my head, swore two or three bad oaths, and told them, 'The man that doesn't put his hand to the pump, I'll chop his head off.'

They stared at me, then moved off in a dogged sulky way and I kept my eye on the sea-lawyer and said, 'Lay hold of that pump handle, Pitch.' I remember now that was the name he used to go by. He looked at me and I said, 'Or by God, I'll chop your head down.' I wasn't going to chop his head down. I was going to chop down between the shoulder and the neck on the left side. He saw it in my eyes and went to work.

And now I'll say something about fighting at sea. At sea you meet some hard cases, especially before the mast. I knew I was pretty tough, and once I'd got to sea and was knocking round the fo'c'sle when I was about seventeen, eighteen, I could take my part against any of the bullies, there's always one, and sometime I got licked, but licked them more oftener. But once you become an officer: well, unless you can use your fists, you might as well look for a thousand dollars in the street as look for a mate's berth.

The crowd would get together first day out and say, 'We've got that "bucko mate" Barnes, we'll have to keep that fellow quiet.' You wouldn't be many hours at sea before one of them would say, 'Hey, who are you talking to?'

You'd say, 'What do you mean?'

They'd say, 'Aw, you're only a chaw-mouth.' And that was the word, 'chaw-mouth', and then you'd start. If you were getting a licking the skipper might stop it. But that one you were fighting was only one out of ten or fifteen, and seeing you licked the rest now wanted a go, and you'd have to fight almost them all before the voyage was over.

I was mate on a ship called the *Peggy*, and saw a man in a long Ulster coat jump aboard and throw his bag on the deck. I thought, 'He's a decent-looking fellow,' then learned he was Wildcat Martin, turned out of his last ship for badly beating another foremast hand. I told the captain, but Martin had had his advance, and the captain wasn't going to lose that. We made Brazil, then

Barbados for molasses, then it was Montreal for orders. It was spring, and I wanted to paint the ship. I mixed some white paint for the yards, and, as each man came along, I gave them a brush and pot. Martin was the last.

I said to him, 'Bill, here's your pot.' He took the brush from me, begins twisting it in his fingers, then throws in down, saying, 'I can't paint with that damn thing!'

I'd never spoke cross to him, and now said, 'Bill, that's all I've got left. You'll have to do your best.'

'Damned if I will! You're only a chaw-mouth!'

I hauled off and struck him. He wasn't expecting I'd hit him so quick. He stumbled, but wasn't down a second but was up again. Then we were at it like two dogs. The captain ran out of his cabin, shouting, but I told him, ' Stay clear! This is going to the finish!' Now the crew gathered round, so I shouted, 'Show fair play, boys!' and we started again. We fought up and down that deck for a quarter of an hour and in the end I couldn't get up, and Martin couldn't, either. Finally, I struggled to my feet and says, 'Come on.' But he couldn't. I walked away, then turned and said, 'Don't blame me, Martin. Saucy dogs get dirty jackets!' He never answered, but didn't bully as much in the fo'c'sle after that, and at Montreal asked for his discharge.

The other memorable one was in the *Seretha*, Mort Murphy, the riverhead fighting man and the biggest drunken blackguard in St John's. I noticed him immediately we were towing out, kicking a young fellow named Power. I told him to stop and we began. It was another dogfight and he was all but beaten when the captain stopped it. I was walking away, and next minute there was splash, and Murphy had jumped overboard and was swimming for the harbour wall.

Twenty-five years later I was third officer on the *Egremont Castle*. We'd loaded human hair and silver in the Far East, the most valuable cargo ever left China in one ship – and we finally got to Boston and anchored. Next morning the stevedores were there bright and early getting the booms out, and the hatches ready to unload. At number three there was a big fellow shouting orders. He recognised me just as I did him, and came running along the deck with both hands out. It was Murphy.

He called his gang, and says, 'Look boys! The only man that ever gave me my Waterloo! Licked me on the deck of the *Seretha*!' We had a long talk, and he was now married and that evening invited me to his house where we spent the first part of the evening with his wife, and the fine young woman who was his daughter, educated and accomplished, played the piano for us. After that we went round the beer shops and everywhere he would tell them how we fought and I beat him square; a changed man, and now very comfortable.

To get back to the *Corinne*. Things were now critical. It was still pump day and night, and I knew sooner or later they'd get desperate and try to have me – even if one got killed doing it. And I also knew that if they took the ship, they'd sink her after launching the jollyboat. Then they'd try for shore – now a couple of hundred miles away – taking me along to bleed me and drink my blood, because if I reached shore alive they'd be up for mutiny.

But now we reached the trades and began to move among bunches of seaweed, some big as a table, some like a book. These bunches hang together, and can stop a ship in a light wind. And that night we got a suck on the pump! The seaweed must have got into the hole and plugged it: you'd be surprised at the pressure on a ship's bottom only four foot under the waterline – it would knock you down like a fire hose. So now we were making no more water than in St Thomas harbour.

I gave them some rest – they need only pump every hour. I now wanted to be as good to them as I could, so told the mate and second mate to give them no work but pumping. I made much of them, and gave them grog often, and they were all right. All hands wanted to forget the axe business.

We passed Cape Hatteras, but kept tight to the coast in case her seams opened again. After Montauk Point I decided to go through Vineyard Haven Sound to shorten the voyage. I had no charts but chanced it, even against a north headwind. I saw a little harbour called Holmses Hole and put in to see if I could get a chart, and by God, there was a ship's chandler there, Eldridge, who had one made by a member of his own family. I paid a pretty good price but it was a damned good chart and I was damned pleased to get it. I then spent a pleasant evening with him and his family, and next morning presented him with a dozen coconuts.

We set off again and now, with the wind from the north, it was becoming cold. None of the crew was out of the West Indies before, and they all thought they would die. One boy was just outside the cabin door trying to polish the binnacle. His teeth were chattering and striking each other as if one would smash off the other. I asked what was the matter.

'I got de fever, sir.'

'What fever?'

'I dunno, sir. Bite me no see 'em.'

He meant, you know, the cold was biting him and he couldn't see it. I looked at him. If you were dying you would have to laugh: on his a head a skullcap, and the leg of an old stocking with the foot cut off and pulled down over his face, with two round holes in it to see out of; a waistcoat that had a gap of six inches from button to button, and was tied about with old tarred spunyarn; a small coat that only came half way around him, while his legs were parcelled up with strips of sail canvas hitched all over with that same spunyarn. Around his shoulders was a piece of old woollen house curtain with red and yellow tassels hanging from its edges.

I put my hands on the waistcoat and asked, 'What's this?'

'Confirmation jacket, sir.' I could stand it no longer, I roared laughing.

Mr Simmonds came along, 'What's de matter, Cap?'

I waved a hand, went down to my room, and filled a tumblerful of rum. I brought it up and gave it to Simmonds, and, I tell ye, it disappeared quick! I took it back down, filled it again, gave it to the boy. He had to hold it with two hands to get it to his mouth, and while he was drinking the glass played a jingle on his teeth. All the rest of the crowd had been down the hold and were dressed in old rags, cloths, old pieces of canvas, like a lot of dead Egyptian mummies just out of their coffins. I would not have needed an axe to kill them that day. I gave them all rum and they were delighted.

The worst was over now and I got around the land and up to Cape Cod and steered for Minot's lighthouse and got a pilot. We took a tug for the last part and anchored about 2pm. Next morning I reported to Marvelle's agent, a Mr Hoxie, State Street, Boston.

'Captain Barnes!' he says. 'Glad to meet you. Ship and cargo all right?'

'The cargo is all right,' I said. 'But the ship leaks and will have to go into dock.'

'Marvelle never said anything in his letters,' he replied. I thought this strange, but said nothing. 'Well,' he then said, 'bring her into Long Wharf. I've sold part of the cargo. How did you ship your crew? For the run up, or the voyage?'

'The voyage.'

'Well, I can get you a cargo of ice to take back down, but it won't be ready for a month. If you could pay them off now it might be better. You might sound them out.'

I did so, and they were delighted. That night they all got drunk, and when I came aboard at 11pm were having a great time in the fo'c'sle. One came along and said they wanted a drink with me before they left. I never like to hurt anyone's feelings, and knew they meant well, so went forward. They had all kinds to drink – whisky, brandy, beer. We all shook hands and I had a drink with them.

As there was no cooking on board, I ate in restaurants and charged the ship ten dollars a week. I had her pumped every evening, drawing money from Hoxie. I slept aboard and never touched my wages. I wrote to Marvelle at St Thomas regarding the cargo of ice, but never got an answer.

Every morning I would go to Hoxie's office, read the newspaper, and wonder to Hoxie why I had no letter from Marvelle. Hoxie would just smile, a curious sort of smile which I didn't understand, and which he had no intention I would.

After five weeks there was no sign of the ice or any letter, and one morning, up at the office, Hoxie says, 'Captain, I have written two letters to Mr Marvelle with no reply. He owes me five thousand dollars for two previous cargoes and I can get no satisfaction.'

Shortly after this, I wished him, 'Good morning,' and made my way back to the ship. As I approached, I saw a man sitting up aft reading newspaper, and with his coat off. I climbed aboard and he said, 'Excuse me, are you the captain?'

'Yes,' I said.

'Then I'm sorry to tell you, captain, I'm the marshal's man.' I stared at him and he pointed towards a paper pasted on the mainmast. I read it and found Hoxie had put a lien on the ship. I told the marshal that Hoxie was my agent, and that I'd need to speak to him.

I opened my cabin and told the marshal to make himself at home, then jumped ashore and caught Hoxie as he was leaving the office. I asked him about the lien. He said, quite cool, that Marvelle owed him five thousand dollars, and that Marvelle had written back to say the *Corinne*'s cargo was worth more than that. But, Hoxie, told me, the cargo was water-spoilt and would not cover what was owed.

'How come you never told me?' I asked

'Oh, captain, then I would have had to pay you your wages, and I'm owed too much already.'

'So!' I said. 'My wages? Who does pay them?'

'That is now in the hands of the United States Marshals.'

I said, 'This ship is a Danish ship and I'll need to go to the Danish consul.'

'As you wish, captain.'

The consul's name was Lutes, and he read out that Danish law said that on a Danish ship being seized the crew take all prior claim before other creditors. We talked it over, and he pointed me towards a lawyer called Brown. I saw right away Brown was a smart fellow who knew a deal about shipping. I told him now that I wanted to put a lien on her.

'Look,' he says to me, 'you do that and your wages stop today. You're still aboard?'

'Yes.'

'Then stay there and you'll get another month and a half out of her before he can sell her. Look for the advertisement in the paper that she's about to be sold, then I'll go up and put a lien on for you.'

We hung on until two days of her selling, then Brown put a second lien on her. The day of the sale the rain was coming down pell-mell, and not many people showed. The *Corinne* was knocked down for $430; if I'd had the money I'd have bought her myself. She was given away – that money wouldn't have bought half her sails.

The case came up in court before Judge Nelson; I was there and my lawyer and Hoxie's lawyer. Hoxie was not there. Brown, my lawyer, says, 'It's the law of Denmark that the captain is the same as the crew.' The judge wanted the Danish consul. He said that in America the 'officers' and 'crew' have a claim, but the 'captain' is seen as a part owner, not due anything except pro rata as a creditor.

The consul came up, and the judge asked him about Danish law. The consul said about the crew taking prior claim. Hoxie's lawyer said the consul must swear I was part of the crew. The consul said he had no need, it was the law. The judge said unless he would swear I was part of the crew, he could only give me pro rata as a creditor. The judge was trying to get the consul to swear – encouraging him – but would the consul swear? No. He just said, 'That is the law,' and left the box.

Judge Nelson looked at me. 'Captain, I'm very sorry. I know the ship owes you this money, and you've been working for nothing and risked your life in this vessel. But I can't help you. If the consul had sworn, you would have had your money in full. Now I can only give you pro rata.' That was thirty-two dollars, instead of four hundred. But I took it, and went away, and got blind drunk.

10. Breakers under the lee, *Vidonia* – my last sailing ship, *Mystery* – ashore as customs officer – my wife dies – my first steamship – passengers – mules – a negro parson's funeral.

THINGS WERE STILL slow when I met Wilson in the street. He had come out from the west of England and married a St John's woman. He had come out a young man, but was now old and pot-bellied.

'William Barnes,' he says, 'Whhaat are ye dooin?' That's west of England talk.

'Nothing,' I says. 'Not now.'

'Well,' he says, 'I want a mate. You'll come with me?'

I joined him on the *Vidonia*, a three-mast barquentine, fore and aft rigging, though square on the foremast. On the second night out, it was my watch on deck, but I needed something from my cabin and slipped down. Wilson was lying on his bunk and, as he wasn't capable of speaking in a whisper, I heard him talking with the steward, a Liverpool Irishman who I'd got the job.

'Steward,' he begins, 'every night before you turn in,

take the sugar and butter out of the pantry and stow it away. The h'officers come down in the night scoffin' and eatin' and the ship can't afford for men eatin' both all day *and* night. Bread is not so much odds – there's plenty of that.'

The steward come out and sees me. We couldn't talk but he gives me a wink as much to say, 'Dirty old swine.'

Wilson liked his rum. He thought I didn't know when he was drinking, but when he drank he coughed so I always did know. He would have a jug at the back of his pillow so he didn't need to get out of his bunk. He never offered me a drink. But as for work – well, then it was nothing but 'Mr Barnes here' … 'Mr Barnes there' …

We were for Oporto. We'd had no sun for two days and I reckoned we were about fifty miles off the Portugal coast when we picked up a beam wind. It began to blow and rain. Wilson didn't want to go near the land with weather like that so he told me to wear her round and put her stern to the land. Only he didn't say it like that. He was a smutty old fellow, with a dirty way of saying things.

I just said, 'All right, sir.'

He looks at the glass, and says, 'I think we'll have more before we have less.' And I thought so, too.

We shortened down, and the seas got mountains high, and the wind veered, and suddenly we were off the Highlands of Viana, mountains right to the beach,

Oporto sixty miles south, Cape Finisterre eighteen miles
north. This was very dangerous, a lee shore, and if a
ship goes against the rocks there's no getting out boats
or anything, two strikes and she's gone, everyone
drowned together. Now the wind began properly and
the sea got up more, and we began to drive towards
those cliffs at about two miles an hour, whatever sail we
set. It was about two in the morning. By the time
daylight came we had a hurricane, and at 10am a sea
came aboard and washed the binnacle and compass
adrift, smashed in the galley door, stove in the side of
the longboat and threw it on top of the jollyboat, and
knocked in a lot of the bulwarks.

Wilson came up half-drunk. 'Mr Barnes,' he says.
'Did that do much damage?'

'Nothing to talk about,' I says.

He gave a set of orders to hove to, then just about
managed to stumble down to his cabin again. I gave
the crew the orders and we're hove to and now at
noon I went down for my watch below, and all this
time we were drifting onto the Viana Highlands. At
4pm I was on deck again, by five it was coming on
dark with a hazy horizon of about four miles. Not like
in cold climates where the land is clear however it
blows. I walked to leeward and saw we were still
driving onto those cliffs. I was standing there about
five minutes when, by God! I thought I got a glitter of
something.

I jumped alongside the fellow on the wheel and said, 'Do you see anything? Look!'

'It's like land,' he says, 'like breakers under the water!' I realised we were in a hell of a tide, and went right down to Wilson's cabin.

'Captain Wilson,' I says, 'There's breakers under her lee.'

'Whaat? … Nonsense!'

'Nonsense be damned! Come up and look.'

'We were fifty miles h'off this morning. She couldn't have drifted that much.'

'There's two of us sees them plain,' I told him. 'We got to do something and damn quick.'

'What can we do, mister? The ship's hove to.'

'You're going to watch yourself going against the cliffs?'

'Well,' he says, 'whaat can we do?'

'Put sail on! It might sweep the decks, but she'll tear herself clear towards Oporto where there's sandy beaches to get under us. Get up and have a look!' Then I realised he couldn't because he was drunk.

I went back up myself, thinking I'd rather drown on deck. Then down to the bosun's room – young Teddy Whaite. He was sleeping. 'Teddy,' I said, 'Get out quick!' I went back up, and when he joined me I pointed, and said, 'Look! Viana!'

'And we're hove to,' was all he said.

I told him I'd been down to talk to the old pig (as I

called him), that we needed to put sail on to send her south to a sandy beach, but that he'd turned his back on me, beastly drunk.

Teddy called the hands at the run, scared as I was. I told them what I intended to do and they went to work and loosed the sails and she made three or four leaps like a fellow getting kicked in the backside, or a wild horse getting the whip. And now she began to move and I saw the wake beginning to straighten out on the quarter. At least it would now take her eight hours to go ashore, instead of four. I began to walk the deck scratching and itching. I wanted more sail on, but was frightened, but said to myself, 'If she goes, what's the odds. We're drifting shore anyway.' So I called to set the topsail and take a reef out of the mainsail. I put a rope round myself and made myself fast to the mizzen rigging, and told the men to go down into the foc's'le. She began jumping lively now, but with the wake astern – nearly straight with the ship. And now the glass began to move upwards, and the wind to lull a bit, and when daylight came I set more sail, and she began to hop even livelier, and I knew there would be no lee shore now. Then the sun came out and the weather settled and I set every stitch on her. It was about 7am.

At eight his Holy Worship came up, just about sober enough to be out of his bunk. 'Good morning, Mr Barnes,' he says.

'Good morning, Captain Wilson.'

'The wind's down a bit,' says he.

'Yes,' I agree. 'It is.'

He looked aloft. 'You haven't got too much sail on her have you?'

'Can't you see for yourself?' I says.

'Whaat did you mane coming down last night to say she was drivin' on the breakers?'

'I wonder you don't remember, sir,' says I. 'And it was yesterday afternoon, Wilson, not last night, and the ship nearly in the Viana breakers.' (No 'captain' now)

'Whaat did you do?'

'Put sail on. What you were too drunk to understand to do. And look! No breakers now! Just a beautiful sandy shore.'

'I think you're exceeding your duties, mister,' he says to me.

'Well, Wilson, you fell a damn way short of yours last night.'

'Any more from you, mister, I'll send you to your room.'

'Any more from you, Wilson, and I'll put you in irons!' Well, gentlemen, sirs, you never saw a man go down those stairs quicker.

About noon he came up, pretending he forgot what he'd said to me, and what I'd said to him. An hour later calls me, and says, 'Mr Barnes, damn it, man. Sit ye down and let's forget what passed between us.'

'Wilson,' I says, 'I've been with fellows like you

before. And have never injured one of them, if they don't try to injure me.'

'Barnes!' he says, 'Shake hands!' And I did, but knew the old swine hated me all the same.

We made the entrance of the River Douro just before dark, Oporto, a fine city, being twelve miles up it. At the entrance of the Douro they built a breakwater and beautiful harbour called Port Lexious, but which we call the New Harbour. Here you can wait for orders, rather than beat round outside. Generally, you run up your flags, and if the signal station has received your orders, they turn up 'Proceed Lisbon' or 'Proceed to Malaga' or whatever.

I asked Wilson if he was anchoring in the New Harbour, and he said he'd never been there at night. I said I could put her in, but he said he would rather wait outside and beat about. That night it blew up again another howling sou'wester and we had to run back out to sea, and lost our stanchions, boats, etc, and Wilson decided he had to jettison some of the cargo. I was nearly mad with vexation. I had to turn the men to, the cargo had to be thrown overboard, the ship was now smashing herself up and lying deep. And we were drifting back to Viana again. It was heart-breaking to think we might be lying in Lexious at anchor.

We rode out the gale, but it was five days before we were back in Oporto Bay. In Oporto we found the schooner, *Mayflower*, who had left St John's after us, but who was already in a week and discharged, and who knew they'd given us a terrible beating.

Now Wilson began to go ashore every night, coming back about 11.30pm half-stewed. The *Vidonia* lay off about thirty feet, the water being too shallow to allow her to lay alongside. This meant keeping a boat onshore ready for Wilson when he made it back, and showing a light in the rigging, and a man to watch for his return. This latter was a jolly old fellow, Doyle, who'd sit in the galley waiting for Wilson to come to the edge of the pier and climb in the boat.

The night in question was very cold, and I'd been sitting reading in my cabin. Getting uncomfortable I went up to the galley. 'Doyle,' I says, 'Any hot coffee?'

'Yes, sir,' he says and fills me a mug. We talk of old times for a bit, then he said, 'That old rooster' – they all hated Wilson – 'will be along soon.'

And sure enough now we heard him, '*Vidonia* ahoy!'

Doyle prepared to go on deck to receive Wilson, and, not thinking Wilson would hear me, I said in joke, 'Aw, grease the ladder and let him drown.'

But he did hear me, and when he came on, he walks up and down for a bit on the poop, then says, 'So, mister. You'd like to see me drown?' I said nothing. 'All right,' he says, 'that goes in my log book tonight. That fellow Doyle is a witness. I'll have you before the consul tomorrow, and you'll be sent back to Liverpool in irons, and have your certificate taken from you.'

'Look out it won't be yourself goes back in irons,' was my reply.

At ten the next morning Wilson was up the consul with the whole rigmarole, and the following day I get a note from the consul to come ashore, and when I got to his office Wilson was there, pretending to read a newspaper.

The consul and I were pretty good friends, and when he saw me, he says, 'So it's you, Barnes,' surprised to see me mate rather than captain.

'Yes,' says I, and we shake hands.

'Well,' says the consul, 'a very serious charge – if true.'

'It's true, Consul,' cries Wilson. 'And he can't dispute it!'

'That will do, Wilson,' says the consul. 'Wait until I speak to you.' The consul had read through Wilson. 'Now,' he says to me, 'Captain Wilson has accused you of telling the watchman, Doyle, to grease the steps of the boarding ladder so he, Captain Wilson, would go overboard and drown … Mr Barnes?'

'Consul, it was said in a joke. Do I look like a man who would allow a thing like that to happen?' I told him everything, and could see he was trying hard not to laugh outright.

He said, 'Barnes, obviously you were not in earnest – otherwise, of course, you would not have said it loud enough for him to hear.'

Wilson could keep quiet no longer. 'Consul, if you don't send him to England, and take his certificate, I will write myself to the Board of Trade!'

Before the consul could reply, I says, 'He wants to take my certificate and send me back prisoner, but I'll tell you what happened off Viana and it's his you'll want.' And I told all: Wilson in his bunk, drunk as a pig; me on deck continually for thirty hours, no food or sleep. That, if I'd have listened to Wilson, neither he, nor I, nor the crew, would have any flesh on our bones as we'd all be at the bottom of sea. Wilson said it was all lies – he was not drunk.

'If you weren't,' says I, 'then it's worse. Because then you're a coward.' I asked the consul to send for every man on the ship to see what Wilson would have to say in front of them.

The consul says, 'I believe you, Barnes. But I think the best way is for you two fellows to shake hands and be friends.'

I said I was willing to do this. The consul now called on Wilson, and he came over and shook. But I knew he'd rather be putting a knife into my heart. After we left, and were going down the steps, the consul called me back, and told me every time Wilson came to Oporto there's trouble, and to do the best I could till I could get clear of him.

There were no more rows after that. We went to Malaga, then Cadiz to load salt for home. It was spring, and we met ice three hundred miles off the coast of St John's. With a wooden ship with a copper bottom, we could not enter it as it would strip us. Instead we dodged around – St Pierre, Placentia Bay, down around Cape Race, and finally into St John's. The anchor had hardly struck when I was over the side. My final words to him were, 'Goodbye, Wilson. Remember me!'

My last sailing ship was the *Mystery*, an old vessel which worked in the sea like a basket. Nearly everything worn or played out, which made the trip so much longer; drift from port to port, load and unload; until we finally took salt from Figueira for St John's. When we got back my owner said he was well pleased with my work and gave me a present of twenty dollars.

I had a look round but the ships on offer were not the same sort of ships I'd sailed, so I said to my wife I might go over to England to see what they had there. She said if I wasn't satisfied, why didn't I go into the Custom House? That isn't easy, as customs officers had to be appointed by the executive assembly. I spoke to a few members, and they said that there were hundreds trying to get those jobs, but added that as my father and family had given more employment than any others to the people of Newfoundland, I would be all right, and I was appointed.

I was there about two years and my wife died. I was sick of it anyway as I was used to an active life, and now my daughter got married, and she and her husband went into Canada to live, and five of my other children wanted to go with her. So I sold off what we had, and gave her the money, and moved myself to Montreal, moved to be there for them.

Then I went to Furness Withy and applied for an officer's job in one of their steamers. I've never been in a sailing ship since.

After cutting my steam teeth with Furnace Withy, I joined the Quebec Lines *Korona* and halfway across the Atlantic, in the middle of the Gulf Stream, we ran into one of the worst nights I ever experienced at sea. Huge seas, howling winds, and carrying 128 mules and a saloon full of passengers, and the ship awash. I had the eight to midnight, and about half ten there was a terrific clap of thunder with a fork flash of lightning that knocked me about ten feet. And just as the man at the wheel jumped down the stairs, the captain jumped up to tell me one of the passengers was in his cabin saying how bad things were in the saloon, and could I go down. Then added that he'd heard that passengers calmed down when they heard the officers swearing, because they thought if the ship was going to sink they would hear the officers praying rather then swearing.

I made it down to the main deck which was awash from rail to rail. I was right up to my neck in water, dragging myself along by the safety lines, and when I got to the saloon I stood before the door for a time, then started in accompanied by all the choicest oaths I could think of.

What sight! It was full of water, and half-naked women rolling about on the floor and on top of each other. Some hanging on to the legs of the cabin table, some to the handles of the doors; some laughing, some crying, some praying, some hysterical. There was also the tin cans they hang on a hook on the side of the berths for passengers to vomit into with seasickness. These were being thrown all over, hitting all the passengers.

I now yelled in my 'dirty night at sea' voice, 'What the hell is the matter here!? Is it a lunatic asylum!?'

One old piece, her head was all white, was in her night clothes and had rolled out of her bunk, and was on her knees hanging onto her stateroom door. Every time the ship would roll she would swing to with it, and then be dragged back when it rolled the other way. Now she said, hanging onto her door knob. 'Are we to be lost, mister?'

'Lost! This is only a squall, ma'am!'

'I rolled out of the top berth,' said she.

'Then let me put you in the bottom one where you should have been put first.' She was small, light, and thin, and I picked her up easily and put her in the berth and put her back against the side of the ship, and told her to double up her knees and press them against the side of the berth, to hold on with her two hands, and when the ship rolled, to roll against it.

I then went round the others helping where I could,

swearing hard and cheering them up with jokes, until, at last, got a bit of peace and quiet. I roared for the stewards to come and pick up their gear and vomiting cups, but none appeared.

I couldn't be away from the deck any longer so left telling them, 'There is no danger. The sun will shine tomorrow.'

I went back up to the bridge and described what I'd seen, and thought the captain would crack his guts laughing. Down on the foredeck, the mules were all in a pound; their noses were made fast to some kind of stick that ran across the front of them. Some were laying down, some were on their heads, and they were all, I don't know what they call it – 'whinnying' is it? Like a brass band. You felt for the poor devils.

I went down to my room and Jimmy Wade, our chief steward, from Dublin, was there. He was round like a ball, with a red cherry face, and was hairless. I found him on my lounger. He and I were great chums. 'Hello, Jimmy,' says I.

'Oh,' he says, 'isn't it an awful night?'

'I don't see much wrong with it. Anyway, what are you doing here?'

'I couldn't stay aft,' he says, 'I thought the stern was going out of her,' and pulled out a big bottle of whisky.

We had a good drink and I climbed in my bunk and said, 'Aw, lay down and go to sleep.' And next morning he'd disappeared, and so had the gale.

I stayed on the *Korona*, and made second officer, and one trip a black preacher died and it was a good as any Irish wake, shillelaghs and all.

He'd been preaching in New York, but belonged to Barbados, and was going home. He was in steerage, but on evenings when the weather was fine enough, he'd hold prayers on the fore hatch with a big box for a pulpit. All the steerage were coloured people and they would come up and cluster round him at the prayers. After we left St Thomas he contracted a heavy cold, and died between Guadeloupe and Martinique.

The captain knew I'd shot one or two over the side before, and gave me the job of sewing him up. 'You'll have to get him out of steerage,' he said, 'It's too hot down there. Get him up on deck.' Then later, 'You won't be able to do anything with that damn crowd of nigger wenches round. Get the bosun to haul up an old sail and rig it as a tent. Heave it over the main boom and tie it to a ring-bolt so they can't get under it, and close up the lace lines in front. Put two men on duty to stop them going in while you're working on him. We'll have to treat him as some kind of minister even if he is black – treat him with some kind of respect. If not, these people will all be blabbing when they get back home.'

I went and got the bosun, who was half-coloured himself. He was a damned decent fellow, and I said to him, 'I guess you and I are doing the dirty work, so I'll go aft and get the needles and palms, and you get the men to put a spare sail over that foreboom and make a tent.' So we got everything ready, and now I went down into the steerage to superintend getting up the preacher's body. My God! If you could have heard.

'Oh, oh, handle him gently, handle him gently.'

'Aw,' says I, 'shut up and let us do our work.'

'Oh, you blackguards! You blackguards!' as if he were alive. We got him on deck with the crowd all around.

'Get out of this, you hussies,' says the bosun.

'Who you call hussies – you scamp! What way id dat to haul de poor parson about. He is a preacher, he is, aldo he black, he preach as good as de white man.'

'Shut up, damn you. And get out of this or we will heave you overboard with him,' said the bosun, and now they wanted to mob him. I could do nothing, I was laughing so much, and then the captain arrived with a broom to threaten them.

At last we got him in the tent and one old dame sung out, ' Cap, he is a parson, ain't you gwine to shave him and give him a fittin' funeral?'

I roared out again, but the captain whispered, 'Get a razor and shave him.' We laid two boards on some boxes, and straightened him out on them. None of the crew would hand over their razors, so I had to go and get mine.

'Now,' I said, 'we'll get after him and make him look decent.'

'All right,' says the bosun, delighted because he thought I was doing his own colour great respect and all that.

We got into the tent and set to work. He wasn't a bad-looking nigger, you know, what you'd call a well-formed face. I got a cup of soap, and lathered him up. Now the captain, from the bridge, saw all the others trying to get in the tent, getting impudent, wanting to see what we were doing. He came down shouting, 'Get out of there! Get out of there.'

Anyway, when he was lathered up nice and white, I cast my eye down and saw a black face looking at me from under the edge of the tent. She said, 'What you doin' wit dat man?'

I thought to frighten her, so caught him by the nose and drew the back of the straightedge razor across his throat, just as if I'd cut it. She let out a screech and I don't know if she passed out or what.

When he was shaved, we got the canvas round him and sewed him up, the bosun starting at his feet and me at his head. All outside were howling and crying I'd cut his throat. Two of the sailors had sticks keeping them clear. It was good as a theatre or movie.

Martinique was in sight now, where we intended to bury him. They could put him into a coffin there and hold a funeral. But Martinique, you know, is French and Roman Catholic, while the parson was Protestant, and bigoted Protestant too. The purser went ashore to consult the authorities and all the passengers went ashore as well, but only for amusement around the village. They weren't interested in the parson. When the authorities found he was Protestant, oh, they didn't know what he died with, so it was 'Keep him aboard! Keep him aboard!'

We took him back out to sea and buried him three miles from Martinique, that was their strict orders – buried him outside the three-mile limit.

The first mate and I had a good laugh about it all that night, and afterwards they christened me 'The Undertaker'.

11. The Great War – I offer my services to England – five hundred floating French dead – I fall in love with Mary, a German spy – torpedoed on the *Saxonian* – three days and nights adrift – I am credited with a U-boat kill.

IN THE SPRING of 1914 I joined one of Houston's, the *Herminius*, and was in Liverpool when war was declared. What excitement! All the volunteers going enlist! All the talk, 'How long will it last?'

'Oh, three months and we'll have them licked.'

'Three years, more like it,' I said, and they were going to eat my head off. The women in the beer shops were even worse for a fight; over there women go into beer shops same as a man.

'My man is going,' one would say, 'I was up all night getting his things ready.' You had to laugh.

The colonial troops began arriving, my son among them. He wouldn't go in the Navy; his pals were shore chaps, so went with the Army to the Dardanelles. Only thirty of his regiment came out. Then he was sent to

France and was four months in a big battle, Ypres or Mons. He got a blow of shrapnel and was sent to hospital in London for four months; I didn't know, I could have visited him. Later he went with Peary to the North Pole. Peary was known as the 'Big Chief', and my son the 'Little Chief', as he was youngest on the expedition.

I went to the Admiralty offer my services. This old chap full of gilt and stripes and medals asked what he could do for me and I told him. We came to how old I was. 'Sixty-four.' He said I was the oldest man to have come across from 'the other side', but that I was over-age. I said one of my other sons, a captain, had given up his ship to come over and volunteer, and I wanted to do the same. He liked my spirit, and said he'd send for me.

About two days afterwards I got a letter in a long envelope to be at his office 9am sharp next morning. He asked if I was willing to sail as second officer, and I said 'before the mast' if necessary. So he sent me to Waterloo Dock where they would be waiting for me on the *Moreus* – Captain Windsor. Windsor said he was glad they'd sent an older man and would I take a drop of 'Black and White'. So that was all right.

A week later we were mined off Malta. During that war I was mined, and torpedoed twice, in three different ships. One of these was the *Inverbervie*. I was on the bridge one morning just after daylight, after passing through the Aegean Isles. Looking round with my glasses I saw a blue thing off the starboard bow. I gave the glasses to the young fellow on the wheel I thought would have sharper eyes than mine.

He says, 'I don't know. It looks like a buoy, painted blue.' I took back the glasses and made it out to be a dead French soldier in his pale blue coat. Then another. Then another. In the end it was about five hundred, all dead. Some were lying face up, their eyes wide open, their long blue French soldier coats flapping in the water, some had the their mouths open. It was ghastly – the worst sight I ever saw. The captain was named Radcliffe.

I called him and he peeped over, then said, 'Barnes, I can't look at it.' We couldn't stop, and when we got to Malta I heard it was a French transport carrying about six hundred troops that had been torpedoed. The Germans had a submarine base among those little islands and did a lot of damage from it.

Now I'll tell you how I could have been shot as a spy. In 1915 I was on the *Antigone*, from Buenos Aires to Cardiff with wheat. At Cardiff I was unwell and was discharged for a time. I knew Cardiff well, and on St Mary's Street there was a hotel called the Philharmonic where I always stayed when alongside there. The landlady was Mrs Davies, a fine-looking woman of about forty. There was a public bar, and also a private bar for guests at the back of the public bar – you ordered your drinks through a hatch from a girl sitting at a cash desk next to the hatch. This girl was named Mary, who appealed to me in a different way from most: a sort of mellow, silver voice, like putting your hand on velvet, and seemed highly educated. She had Sunday afternoon and night off, and one night in the middle of the week. We'd meet at these times, and I was as much in love with her as I could be.

One day Mary was not there, and I learned that Mary and Mrs Davis had had a big row that morning, that they had their fists up, that Davis had called Mary a 'damned baggage', and Mary had packed her grip and gone. I was in a hell of a state, and walked the streets for four days but never saw her.

I met a chief mate I knew, Thompson, at the shipping office where I was waiting for my replacement discharges to arrive for ones I'd lost being torpedoed. We were talking on the steps when a heavily muffled woman walked past. Thompson said how stately she walked, and thought she'd lost someone in the war because she had a veil over her face.

Thompson left, and I was walking up the street when I passed her again. She was looking at me, but as I don't like to stare at a lady, I ducked my head and walked by. Then I heard 'Barnes!' You can imagine how I jumped. She threw up her veil and was laughing at me.

I asked where she'd been, told her the state she'd had me in. She said she'd been looking for me as well, and we could go to her place, a parlour and bedroom in a house owned by an Irishwoman named Murphy, but that now she was Mrs Mary Welsh, widow of a Liverpool man killed in action. I'd never really asked Mary about her background, always hoping she'd tell me, but now I asked if it was true she was a widow. She wouldn't tell me, but said there were good reasons for being secretive, nor would she tell me what she and Mrs Davis had rowed about.

We got to her new place, and she introduced me to Mrs Murphy, and then set out some wine, whisky, cake and cheese – she had everything there. We ate and had a long talk, and I told her I'd been frightened I'd never see her again. She laughed and said that wouldn't happen, and we went the theatre and I took her home at about 11.30, saw her in, and went back to my room.

This went on, afternoons and evening, and I might as well tell you I told her I loved her better than my life, and she said she loved me. I often think of one night when she said to me, 'Will, if you were to hear something terrible about me would you still love me?' I told her I would love her if all the world ran her down and she flung her arms round my neck and kissed me and began to cry, but wouldn't tell me why.

Now I was having to sail again, which upset her, and she said, 'If you keep going back they'll get you. If only this war was over.'

The next time I went to see her I arrived about 4.30pm – usually it was between three and four thirty.

I knocked on the door. Usually Mrs Murphy would open it with a pleasant face, but this time she closed the door to a slit, and said in a loud voice, 'You've a hell of a cheek coming here!'

I was taken flat aback and said, 'What the hell have I done?'

She opened a bit wider and said, 'You don't know?'

'Know? Know what?'

She looked at me hard, then opened the door fully and invited me in. She told me she was convinced I was innocent, then said, 'You were late round today – just as well. For if you'd been with her at three o'clock, you'd be shot as she will be.' I stared at her, as she went on, 'She's the biggest German spy in England, and, what's worse, comes from a good German family. They were wealthy, and became poor, and she came over as a governess with some big English family and then left them to spy, at least, that's what the men who arrested her told me.' Then Mrs Murphy, one of those good-hearted women at bottom, suddenly burst out crying and said Mary was a nice lady, and she'd liked her very much. Then the tears started running down my cheeks. And if I wasn't crying, I was pretty damn handy to it.

I never found out what happened to Mary, but if I met her tomorrow I would marry her on the spot if she'd have me. Sometimes I almost wish they'd found me with her. As for her spying, she was only doing all she could for her country when it was in trouble, and if you ask me if I still love her, yes I do, twice as much.

I now went back to sea for the duration of the war, and was in nine different ships, one of which was the *Saxonian*. We left London, broke down, went back in for repairs, and were then for Port Arthur to load oil. We reached Bermuda and went in to coal. They'd just finished a new canal they'd cut between two islands to make a shortcut to the coaling station and we were to be the first ship through. They were all on the bridge, the harbourmaster, the captain of pilots, a naval officer. She struck on the starboard side but went through, but on survey they found her bottom plates a little bulged, and a propeller blade broken. The crew began saying she was a hoodoo ship and would never get back to England. On the way back out of this canal we struck again, this time amidships. Anything insured at Lloyd's, if she strikes, she must have her bottom inspected. Well, they sounded, but everything was clear, no water in the wells, so they decided to proceed. Clear or not, all hands were now convinced she was hoodooed.

We ran up the Gulf of Mexico to Port Arthur and loaded kerosene. That night six of the crew dis-appeared. Going home we called at Norfolk, Virginia, to coal, and those that had not deserted so far did so now. Back afloat it was just the usual thing in January, gales of wind and sea. On 6 February we were tidying up the decks, preparing for Manchester docks. We were about two hundred and eighty miles west of the Fastnet lighthouse at noon. At about 4.40pm I met the bosun, Williams, coming along with two paint pots in his hand and we agreed it was getting too dark to work and I went down to my room. I was sitting there smoking when I heard the report of a gun, and feet running over my head. I was in pants and shirt and grabbed my long oilcoat and lifebelt which I tied round my body. I put on my cap and ran out and heard someone call, 'It's a submarine.'

'Bang!' Another shot. Then someone shouting, 'Get the boats out!'

I was on the stern gun and ran aft to it. The gunner was an Irishman called Murphy from Balbriggan. Anything he aimed at he struck. We'd heave an old barrel overboard and he'd catch it a mile and a half away. Now he said, 'B'gorrah! I can't see anything, and will have to go by guess.'

We were catching it fore and aft. The foremast went over, and the side was knocked out of the cabin house. Then a square skylight went about eight feet from me, and then a torpedo struck the engine room and blew everything to pieces and the funnel went overboard. Luckily the engineers and firemen got out, but we knew we were sinking fast.

I said, 'Captain, don't forget your instruments and chart,' and he went into the chart house. We got our boat swung out, and as some of the crew were green-horns, I told the bosun to take the forward fall, and the

Irishman to take the aft. The bosun moved forward and had taken one turn off the pin when he fell – cut in half. A cupful of his hot blood splashed into my face. Next thing I was struck and fell. I was stunned for a few seconds, then up again. My mouth was full of blood. Something had gone in my right jaw, across under my tongue, and out the left side. I looked round and saw five dead, and six wounded. I said for two fellows to load the two halves of the bosun in the boat – I don't know why as I knew he was dead – then get the rest of the wounded aboard. Just as I was getting across the gunwale myself I slipped and fell, giving myself a hernia, though I didn't know this at the time.

We'd rowed about a mile from the *Saxonian* when suddenly up come the submarine next to us. I thought at first it was a whale. The captain appears and sings out in English, 'What ship was that?'

'The *Saxonian*,' said our skipper.

'Where from?'

'Port Arthur.'

'Where bound?

'Manchester.'

'What cargo?'

'Oil.'

'Where's the captain?'

'Here.'

'Get aboard!'

I had my hand on the side of the submarine, *U39*,

fending her off our lifeboat. Our captain stuck out his hand to me, 'Goodbye Barnes.'

'Goodbye, Cap.'

The U-boat captain sings out, 'Steer east-nor'east and you'll be picked up by a destroyer.' He must have known the destroyer was there. Our other boat was picked up next day, but we were three days and nights in ours. The bosun had a sixteen-year-old son in the ship, and it made you feel bad to see him crying over his father's corpse. The old chief engineer says to me, 'See if you can get him back here, he might fall asleep and we can bury the bosun.'

I led the lad aft and he laid down and I covered him with a coat and he fell asleep and we tied the bosun up with some spun yarn and put him over. When the lad woke he began yelling a bit, but we got him quietened down. My face was still bleeding where the shrapnel went through and I tore off the tail of my shirt and tied it round my chin and mouth.

Those three days and nights were terrible. There were twenty-three in the boat, sailors and firemen. Some of the firemen had only a singlet on, and it was intense cold: a north wind, and in latitude 53° N, and in February. The weather, though, was moderate, otherwise we would have swamped: the boat was only about a foot and a half above the surface. Those poor firemen were perishing, and there was one man had as many clothes as he could pile on, so we told him to take off some of them and divide them with the firemen. He objected so we took them off for him and gave them to them who needed them worst. Supplies were a drop of water out of the keg morning and evening, and a little corned beef and two biscuits per man. The first day passed and we saw nothing. Night came and we took turns steering the boat.

The old chief engineer, Norman, had plenty of pluck and asked me to give a song. I gave packet ship 'Dreadnought', everyone joining in the chorus. Then I sang 'Annie Laurie', 'Come Back To Erin', and my favourite – 'Bonnie Loch Lomond'. Some of them began now to lie down, to give up.

'Damn you!' I'd say. 'Are you going to lay there and die? Get up and row!' They'd give me all this old women's talk about how it was no use as the boat was going to swamp. But as God sent it, the wind continued north, the finest and smoothest wind that blows on the Atlantic in winter, but very cold.

Next day nothing again, and now they were beginning to give up. Then our second night, and I knew we could not last to get to land. About 10pm the lookout shouts, 'A light!' We all jumped up to see a green sidelight and white masthead light coming for us. She would pass about a quarter of a mile away. We got out a rocket, waited until she was right abreast, and sent it up. They could see it reflected on our sail and us standing around, and when the glare got out of our eyes she was going away from us. Sometimes, though, a submarine would lie on the surface and stick up a mast with a sail on it and when a ship approached they'd get a torpedo in their engine room, where they always aimed if they could.

To drown our disappointment I struck up again, and about daylight a big nigger fireman said, 'Good God! Dere is a light!' This time it was a steamer going eastward. We took our second to last rocket and sent it up. He ignored us. We had one rocket left.

Daylight came and we had our little ration – it was not enough, but we knew we had to be careful now. The men began to settle in the bottom of the boat and I went round shaking them and telling them to get on an oar. Then the Old Chief and I sat on opposite sides of the boat, sparring with each other, each trying to knock the other's cap off. This kept our bodies warm, but our feet got awful dead. We'd take off our boots and put our feet in the bailing hole – there was always water there – then rub them to bring them back to life.

At 8pm I reckoned we had made about two hundred miles towards the Irish coast. The night passed fine. The third day passed the same way until about 8pm again when a voice called, 'White light! Right ahead!' We got our last rocket and sent it up. She started coming for us. We did not care if she was a German and took us prisoners.

She came up close, and a voice sang out, 'Lower your

sail and come alongside.' She was a British destroyer. Then the voice said, 'All of you that can do so jump up, and we will look out for those that can't.'

The Old Chief managed to haul himself up, and two or three others, but that was all. When the officer came down, I said, 'There's some laying under that sail. We put it over them to keep them warm.' Most of them couldn't move by now. I dragged myself up the ladder, the tail of my shirt still tied across my jaw. The destroyer captain asked if we could walk, but we needed four men to help us aft to the cabin, a plain little cubby with an iron ladder going down into it. The doctor came and examined our feet and bandaged them. He pointed to my chin and examined it and laughed. He said I'd had a narrow escape and that it seemed to be healing all right, and that he'd bandage it by and by. The Chief, Norman, told him I didn't need a bandage as I'd been singing songs all the time with it like that.

The doctor laughed and sent down a boy with a jug of steaming hot rum. The rum did the trick and we slept for the first time in three days. I woke at 7am with the Old Chief snoring like a liner blowing for tugs. He asked why I woke him and I said I thought he was choking. A boy came down with a good meal of ham and eggs and more rum if we wanted it. We asked him to bring down a bottle to save wearing out his boots.

About 8am the captain told us all the men had

survived, and he would be landing us in Bantry Harbour, near Cape Clear. Next thing he ran down to say that he'd received a marconi that there was a fellow forty miles off trying to sink a steamer.

That tin pot began to tremble, and I knew we must be going through the water at forty miles an hour. The Old Chief began to strap on his lifejacket again, and just then the boy came down with a big black bottle of rum and I says to the Old Chief, 'We'll have a good drink, even if it's our last!' I drank half and handed it to him to finish, saying, 'At least we'll enter the other sphere in good spirits.'

About 4pm the captain appeared again and said it must have been a false alarm. He had been steaming round in a hundred-mile circle and had seen nothing; we were now headed for Bantry, and he'd marconied the shore to have ambulances standing by.

We anchored about dusk on a Sunday. The wharf was black with people, and nurses and nuns from the hospital. When we reached the wharf, only the Old Chief and myself could make it up the gangway alone.

We got to the hospital and us officers were put in a ward by ourselves. One of the nurses was a fine-looking girl named Kearney. In the evening when her work was over she would come in and chat with the Chief and I, and I gave her my address in Cardiff and got hers, and would write now and then, and always get an answer.

After four days we were able to proceed to London by

way of Cork and Fishguard. We were paid our wages, but only until the day the ship went down. For what I'd lost I was given a £10 note. I thought this very small because I had lost more than that would replace.

I now paid my old friend, the admiral, a visit. I told him about it all, and he said, 'Are you not frightened to face out again?' I said I'd continue till it was all over.

The last thing I was on before armistice was the *Mary*, a small fishing craft fitted out as a decoy. She had barque sails like all Dogger Bank fisherman carry, and three hidden guns that could be hove up in half a minute. We had three gunners, three sailors, six men in the engine room, two officers, and myself.

We'd anchor and pretend we were fishing but it was two-legged fish we were after. We made two trips that first week but got nothing. Then one night we left Whitby about 6pm and at about eight were twenty miles off the land. I was on the bridge, talking to the mate, when suddenly up comes a submarine four points off our starboard bow. I blew my whistle and roared, 'Guns!' I saw the torpedo coming just as we dropped our false bulwarks and our guns came out. I saw I might have room to slew and strike him, so turned the wheel hard a-starboard quick, and she was going at about ten miles an hour when the torpedo struck our engine room and nearly cut us in two. I knew all who were down there were killed. But we kept slewing round and he was just disappearing when we struck and went right over him.

We were sinking fast, and I had just had time to get the boats out. I saw nothing more of the submarine but knew she was all broke up. Six of our crowd were killed. Two hours later a destroyer came along and landed us in Whitby.

Next morning I went up by train to London to see the admiral once again. He said, highly pleased, 'I would see three decoys like yours go, to have that other thing where you put her.' He got out a chart, and I gave him the position. He stuck a pin with a red flag on it into the chart, then said to me, 'That's yours.'

But it's one I don't care much talking about, because I feel pretty bad. I saw nothing and know nothing. That's all I can say. I don't want to know anything about it. Thinking about it makes me miserable, and I never care to talk about it.

12. 'Reclassed'.

AFTER THE WAR, every summer or so, I'd go up to Bellevue Clinic for an overhaul – to be 'reclassed' as they say when putting a ship into dry dock. But this time I went to the New York Hospital, and the young doctor put me on the table and tapped me all over with a little hammer as if sounding for rotten timbers. He told me I was sound as a block, but as I was adjusting my trousers saw the truss I got from my hernia when we were torpedoed on the *Saxonian* that I wore for the rest of the war, and then two years sailing the Pacific, and now in a New York Hospital after being on shore three years.

This young fellow now told me I was getting on, and it was going to get bigger. I told him sometimes the lump came out but I pushed it in again with my thumb. He said that I'd better have it fixed soon as possible. I asked if I was liable to slip my cable, but he said it was done every day and there was no danger.

Next day, about 5pm I went in. About twelve that night they came with a stretcher, and two fellows took me to another room where there was a table with a glass top. I crawled up on it, and one of them was stropping a razor, and says, 'Take off that gown.'

I told them my operation was next morning, 10am. They replied that they knew and were there to shave me. I replied that I shaved that morning, but they said it was not my face but all over, and that I was full of hair, and every part needed to be shaved or the doctors would send me back down. Well, I was thoroughly disgusted by the time they'd finished – I reckoned I looked like one of those pigs hung up in a butcher's shop that you see.

I dreaded what was coming next day and if I'd've known what was really going to happen I would have been out of there. About 10am the same two fellows came again and loaded me on a sort of hand-barrow, and as we passed some folks in a hallway one said, 'Look, they're bringing up a dead man.'

I raised my head and shouted, 'Don't you believe it!', which gave them a hell of a fright.

We got in an elevator, and up to the top of the house under a big skylight and I was laid on a table. Dr Dass was the doctor, about fifty, and he told me that they were not going to put me under chloroform because they could see I was still very strong and that people like me coming out of ether sometimes struggle and rip everything that's been done to pieces. He said he had been a sailor, and so he knew I could stand pain, and to do the best I could.

I said to him, 'All right, Doctor. And when you begin to cut I'll begin to sing.'

The two fellows got hold of my arms, although I told them I wouldn't stir, and he went back to his bench and began to rattle his tools; when I heard this my blood began to freeze. He came across with the knife and as soon as I felt it touch my belly I began to sing – 'The Dreadnought' again. And while he kept cutting I kept singing, making it louder whenever I got a hard dash of pain. It felt at times as if there was a dozen big rats in there hauling things about. They finally put in the last stitch, and I stopped singing to find I'd had an audience of all the nurses in the hospital who'd come to hear me. They took me back to my cot, and one by one the nurses came and shook hands with me, and said they thought I was great. I was out after eighteen days, and as I was going Dr Dass wanted the music and words to 'The Dreadnought'.

I said there was no written music – it was composed in the fo'c'sle of that particular ship, but that I'd write out the verses and chorus for him, and then I'd come to his office and teach him to sing it, and I did. And his job is as good now, six years later, as the day he did it.

And now. Well, now I've been ashore nine or ten years, and often get the enquiry, 'What do I do all the time?'

When I first left I went working in the fruit line which gave me pocket money and kept clothes on my back. While doing that I got knocked down by a big cargo truck on Greenwich Street. I'd just come up Jane Street and met an old friend, Tim Sullivan. We were on the corner and ten foot into the kerb, but this great big truck comes across and catches me in the left shoulder and Sullivan as well. It didn't stop, and no one had the sense to take the number. I was laid up for about a week with that one.

I lost that job and couldn't get another – could get nothing – but last year was taking a walk, and came on Abingdon Park on Twelfth Street. I sat by the statue erected to the boys of Greenwich Village who fell in the war, and filled my pipe. Then I noticed a lady opposite who seemed to be working at a paper and looking up every now and then. I thought to myself, 'She's drawing a picture,' and that I didn't want to be in it. So I moved to a bench nearer her – the one next to her was empty and unlike some, still had all its rungs. And now I began looking over her shoulder at what she was drawing. She smiled and said I seemed interested. I thought she might think I was one of them who might be trying to get acquainted with her like they do in those parks, so just said, 'I thought maybe you'd put me in the picture and I'd as soon be out of it.'

She laughed and we got acquainted and she said she thought I looked like a sailor and asked if I'd been sealing and whaling. I said I had, and told her a few things about that, and about the war. Then a gentleman came up who she introduced as her husband, and she put on her cloak and wrote her name and address on a piece of paper, and invited me to visit them. I'd been in New York ten years, and this was the first time I'd ever been invited into anyone's house.

I went to see them a few days later, and it got like I was one of the family. Then they said I ought to write a book. I laughed at first, then thought about it, then started. I wrote in pen and ink in those composition books – ten books in all. Later I spoke most of the stories into a Dictaphone – so what's here is a combination of both.

I began to be a bit of an artist, too. Oil paintings. Some I sell, but more I give away. I make a few dollars, and painting seems to run in the family as my father's first cousin was the great William Morris of London. At home in St John's we had paintings of my grandfather and Uncle Richard and Uncle John by William Morris.

As well, I have a damned serious notion to go to sea again, a longing to be back out there. I used to take rambles down South Street to see the boats backing out, the fellows on the bridge, the captains and mates. But now I've stopped as it torments me, like a boy looking in at a cake shop window.

Because with me it's always been the sea.

When I made that first trip as a schoolboy, on the *Fleetwing*, my father said to the mate, Morrisy, 'I don't want him to go to sea. So give him a damn good putting through!' And Morrisy did, but also told me what my father had said. So when I came home my mother gave me a couple of kisses, while my father shook hands (he wouldn't kiss me – I suppose he was ashamed of the act).

Then he looked at me sideways, and said, 'Well, Will, how did you like the sea?'

'Father,' I said, 'I'm delighted! Jingoes. It's grand!'

And now, if I was young enough, I'd go back this minute. What I like about it, is that it's not humdrum, not monotonous – there's always excitement. It's all about change. You're getting to a port you've never been before next day, and it's like you're living in the thoughts of going to a big new circus tomorrow night, that kind of thing. But ashore? The same darn thing all the time. A man sits down to work, goes home, gets his tea, goes to bed; gets up in the morning, same thing over and over again. But at sea – you don't ever know what's coming: a fight among the sailors, a man washed overboard, a man falling from aloft. People ashore: I have often looked at them with scorn.

I got a berth in Snug Harbour about six months ago, and was sitting there, and there are lots of old fellows spinning yarns, and one comes over and says, 'Well, Barnes. I don't suppose we're long for this life, pretty mouldy, into our eighties. Maybe another four years?'

I says, 'A man could make a fortune in four years.'

'By God!' says he, 'I've given up all thoughts of that. My only thoughts now are for my soul and the next world.'

'Aw! Go on with you!' I said

'You don't think about such things?' he then asks me.

'I'm too busy,' I says.

Now he gets on his horns. 'Are you prepared to die?' he asks.

'Prepared?' says I. 'I was prepared since the first day I went to sea! And wasn't afraid.'

'And that's your religion?' he asks me.

'My religion is a sailor's religion,' I says to him. 'And this is my religion: a clear conscience, a sharp knife, and ready to cut at a moment's notice.'

Notes

1. Walker, Meaghan, '"Such a thing as writing a book": The making of William Barnes's autobiography', *Papers of the Bibliographic Society of Canada*, 48:1 (2010).
2. Warburton, George Drought, *Hochelaga; England in the New World* (London, 1846), pp.18ff.
3. Ibid.
4. Thompson, Spencer, *Domestic Medicine and Household Surgery* (London and Glasgow, 1857), pp.219–20.
5. Bone, David W, *The Brassbounder* (London, 1910; 1939 edn), p.223.
6. Melville, Herman, *Redburn.*
7. Brown, J H, *The Shipmaster's Guide* (London, 1845), p.7.
8. Urban, Sylvanus, (ed), *The Gentleman's Magazine* (London, 1745), p.14.

SEAFARERS' VOICES

A new series of seafaring memoirs

This new series, Seafarers' Voices, presents a set of abridged and highly readable first-hand accounts of maritime voyaging, which describe life at sea from different viewpoints – naval, mercantile, officer and lower deck, men and women – and cover the years 1700 to the 1900s, from the end of the Mediterranean galleys, through the classic age of sail to the coming of the steamship. Published in chronological order, these memoirs unveil the extraordinary and unfamiliar world of our seafaring ancestors and show how they adapted to the ever-demanding and ever-changing world of ships and the sea, both at war and at peace.

For more details visit our website
www.seaforthpublishing.com